MW01113537

"This is the only book which gives a detailed account of the "Beltway Sniper" from a grassroots perspective. It is meticulous, thought-provoking, and easy to read. Eric Penn is not afraid to see the facts outside of mainstream media. In this book he takes on the 'Shadow Government' and Secret Societies."

-Andrew Nevins

"I have not been educated in prestigious universities, nor do I profess to be a scholar of any particular subject. However, I have eyes to see, ears to hear, and a brain to think. All of my senses inform me that the media and government work hand and hand to keep the people blind, deaf, and dumb. The so-called elitist controlled press will never write something as straightforward and controversial as Psychology of Killing. Therefore, I stand alone to make sure you have information that some hope you will never find."

-Eric Penn

# Psychology of Killing:

## What Drove John Allen Muhammad to Kill?

Eric Penn

authorHOUSE™

1663 LIBERTY DRIVE, SUITE 200
BLOOMINGTON, INDIANA 47403
(800) 839-8640
WWW.AUTHORHOUSE.COM

© 2005 Eric Penn. All Rights Reserved.

All rights reserved. No part of this book may be reproduced in any form or by any electronic or mechanical means, including information storage and retrieval systems, without permission in writing from the Author, except by a reviewer, who may quote brief passages in a review. Any members of educational institutions wishing to photocopy part or all of the work in an anthology should send their inquiries to Eric Penn.

First published by AuthorHouse 11/22/05

ISBN: 1-4208-7006-8 (sc)

Printed in the United States of America
Bloomington, Indiana

This book is printed on acid-free paper.

Esoteric Card designed by Eric Penn

# TABLE OF CONTENTS

**322**

**15 Candidates
The Fire Triangle**

# DEDICATION

*This book is dedicated to people who are not afraid to challenge "THE BEAST." But not to those who kill innocent people in THE NAME OF RIGHTEOUSNESS.*

*People who kill innocent people in THE NAME OF RIGHTEOUS-NESS will not see paradise; They will burn in hell as infidels instead.*

*"There is a thin line between righteousness and insanity. The world is fighting over philosophical ideas that cannot be substantiated through science and cannot be solidified with WAR. It is called religion. It is called democracy. Mankind has fought over these theories for thousands of years, and they will continue fighting until the masses wake up, or until the radiation comes down."*

Quote by Eric Penn

## THE ESOTERIC KILLER

During the sniper investigation forensic specialist were trying to determine an appellation for the type of killer they were searching for, the author of 'Psychology of Killing' has named him "The Esoteric killer." This name is to be used whenever referring to the "sniper" by media, educators, and others from this point onward. The author thanks you in advance for your cooperation. An "esoteric killer" incorporates symbols and mysticism into his crimes, symbols that the average person fails to comprehend. The "tarot card" was such a symbol, and it took the criminal act into the metaphysical realm of investigation. The Zodiac Killer would also be classified as an "esoteric killer." Governments who take orders to kill from secret societies, like Skull and Bones, also fall under this classification. You are about to embark on a journey that promises to change the way you see the world. This book will take you places your mind is afraid to go. If you fear the shadow government I suggest that you put this book down right now! Very few people understand the clannish initiation of Skull and Bones. Bloodline is of utmost importance in that Black Lodge of International Freemasonry. The violence you see today is directly related to the decisions "The Wise Men" made years ago to produce a "Psychology of Killing" in the general population. The reason they deemed it "wise" to manage and manipulate murder around the globe was to curb the population, which their demographers predicted would swell to six billion people by 2005. Thomas Robert Malthus (1766-1834) would be pleased with the "Psychology of Killing" that is about to engulf the Middle East, Africa, and Asia. The Brotherhood of death has no qualms about dropping bombs on countries that refuse to allow Caucasian Knights from the hood to dictate the pace of their progress. In this book, you will discover how violence is bigger than the individuals who commit the malicious act, and it serves the purpose of the New World Order. There are some crimes that graduate to the level of esoteric intelligence. The sniper card above indicates a criminal act that has elevated to the esoteric state. Since there is no agency to investigate this type of crime, I have taken it upon myself to take a closer look into the mind of a wicked nation, a wicked act, and a vicious plan. A Nation that mass produces wicked people.

# SKULL & BONES

When the first shootings took place in Montgomery County, Maryland, on October 2, 2002, there was no indication that the rampage would last for three more weeks, nor was there any idea how long the killer had been executing vengeance on unsuspecting targets. All of us were aware that something had gone awfully wrong that day. But we struggled with what was happening that day, and it was hard to put a face on it. All eyes were glued to the television, waiting, anticipating, trying to figure out what the snipers next move would be, and what type of mission was he on? Every person I knew was in a state of absolute fear! The region I resided in moved around in an ultra-paranoid state of mind. The President of the United States of America was updated hourly, as the events unfolded, and body bags were carried to the state medical examiner to determine cause of death. Whoever was responsible for the truculence that day was a master shooter capable of killing with one shot at long ranges and he did not care who got the next bullet! He was extremely self-assured, and willing to accept the likelihood of getting caught, because he killed in the flow of traffic. He was on a mission! Whoever it was, he was dead serious!

Investigative and detailed work would be required to figure out how long the sniper had been killing, and maliciously wounding human beings, who were simply going about their daily routine, trying to eke out a living in an economically uncertain nation. A nation already devastated by the crumbling of the World Trade Center, the Oklahoma Bombing, and anthrax delivered to the seat of the Capitol. A nation scarcely hanging on economically after being attacked Pearl-Harbor-style in New York, Washington D.C, and Pennsylvania. As a matter of fact, the nation was in trouble economically, spiritually, and politically before 911; still, 911 served to further eviscerate a weak country.

The sniper scare of 2002 would cause all those insecurities to resurface. Once again people were dying for apparently no reason and the media covered the stories like a President's inauguration or State of the Union address! Psychologist would have to see their clients more during the Beltway Sniper scare, and reassure them that life would soon return to normal. The truth of the matter was that Sociologist and Therapist alike understood that life would never return to normal after September 11, 2001. Now the sniper situation caused stress levels to increase tremendously as the world watched in awe, the same kind of nervous tension people felt watching planes hit the World Trade Center! I live in Virginia, the geographic area where many of the killings took place, and I felt that same uneasy apprehension.

In the meantime, these crimes had to be solved if normalcy was to return to the streets of America anytime soon. Something had to be done to stop the killing! A team of experts gathered to decrypt the crime scene in an effort to predict the killer's next move, if possible, or to find some kind of inculpatory evidence that could bring this evil to an end.  It would also take time to figure out exactly what the killer, or killers wanted. Were they part of a bigger conspiracy than met the eye? We do not know for sure, and it might take longer to answer that question honestly. Authorities wondered if the killer was following the *'Declaration of War'* put out by Osama bin Laden. Like many "wanted terrorist," Osama bin Laden used to work with the Central Intelligence Agency, now he is their archenemy. This fact made many people wonder if the sniper was an agent turned bad, or a paid assassin. Were the killings a message from the east, or a note from the west? No one knew for sure.

We do know that the entire *eastern* region of America was paralyzed with fear! Richmond residents, where I am from, wondered if the sniper or snipers would come further south, and start taking shots at its citizens. As I stated above, every one that I know personally was on edge. Gun sales skyrocketed in the region as the level of fear increased in the *eastern* tip of northern America. Many residents had already purchased guns after September 11, 2001. After 911 people felt that America was vulnerable to an invasion from Middle Eastern extremist. After what seemed like years of minimum peace, America felt secure and safe before September 11, 2001. Now the trepidation of the cold war was back again, this time with attacks inside our boarders from a mystery killer, or killers, and once again a feeling that had all of us on edge came forth.

The sniper, or snipers, moved with precision and determination, using the Beltway express and side streets to escape detection. From that 'excited activity' authorities surmised that the killers were "specially trained" in the art of "guerrilla warfare." Guerrilla warfare is a unique style of fighting where a seemingly weaker party (warrior) uses cheap innovations to destroy a more sophisticated enemy from the inside. In this particular art of fighting, patience is the key to victory if one has a carefully worked out plan. When the attacker is patient, the victim becomes impatient. Authorities were scrambling impatiently to solve the case, but there were no witnesses, and initially not enough clues to figure out anything substantial. However, the frequency of the attacks caused one to wonder if the killings were random, and not worked out circumspectly at all, just the sloppy work of lunatics. Is it possible that the locations gave some clue into the motives of the attacks? These criminal acts extended from Maryland to Virginia over a period of three weeks. In the areas where the killings took place it started to feel like Marshal Law was exercised, especially with the dragnet in operation.

It is hard to imagine what mischievous force could produce hatred; hatred so physically powerful that innocent people were slaughtered like pigs in a den of lions. History shows us that groups of men could get together to kill if they felt justified, but rarely do individuals use such brutal force against civilians. Governments (which are groups of men) feel justified to produce and use weapons capable of destroying innocent civilians in the mysterious name of *National Security*, which is a euphemism for *White Power*. However, it takes a certain type of man to use such awful power against innocent people. The mind can convince itself of the legality of unjustifiable devastation against innocent people when a religious or patriotic idea is at stake, or when economic uncertainty is somewhere in the mind playing tricks on the individual. I contend that modern men worships the demon of violence when all else fails, and philosophical ideology is the focus, or motivation that energizes this distorted thinking. The 'psychology of killing' is popular in the corridors of European powers, especially the White House, and when the common people imitate this evil usage of political power, through the use of violence, it is looked upon as primitive. But when Super-powers (America in particular) use violence against sovereign country's like Iraq: violence, too many is seen as justified and excusable. There is an obvious paradox that many people fail to even consider, as if one race of people has the "god-given" right to master the earth with violence if necessary, but other so-called races do not have this right. I say that violence should not be accepted at any level, if it is immoral, or if it is directed at innocent people. If there is a hidden motive to control the *natural resources* of a country like Iraq, then violence is not morally justified, although it is used. When you demand something from your victims it is robbery, not patriotism. When individual criminals, like serial killers, or the snipers show us what administrative violence looks like when used against innocent country's, we are appalled. We should also be disgusted when our government kills innocent people and make demands.

The beltway sniper showed us what vengeance looks like when directed at innocent populations. They did this with the same insanity that Robert Julius Oppenheimer demonstrated when developing the Atomic bomb. The bomb was made to strike fear in the hearts of man. The sniper wanted to strike fear in an already anxious people. Look at the damage done from one rifle and compare it to the potential damage Robert Julius Oppenheimer's weapon caused at the close of World War II. If a nuclear bomb is used in our lifetime the definition of violence will change forever. We will then see it differently and may even realize that violence on all levels is wrong. If we ever plan to live in real peace on earth, then we must study the *'psychology of killing'* on all levels. Examination of violence must start from the top to the bottom. Therefore, this book will not just be about the Beltway Snipers, it will also speak to the violence that governments inflict on weaker nations to rob them of their human dignity, natural resources, and will-power.

## Psychology of Killing

> *"Yahweh saw how great man's wickedness on the earth had become, and that every inclination of the thoughts of his heart was only evil all the time."*
>
> —Genesis 6-5

What causes man to meditate on his destructive powers at the disbursement of his peaceful nature all the time? When insecurity invades the psychology of a man he subconsciously attempts to destroy himself, or his neighbors. His first attempt at destroying himself usually turns into anger at those outside of him. His family is usually the first ones to feel his wrath. That anger is evident in his failed relationships with those closest to him. When everything dear to him flees his fury he finds a target somewhere that can absorb his pain. There is a psychology of killing that is permeating the minds of men as we enter the last days.

Religion and philosophy play a huge part in creating this idea that violence is justified, because religion teaches that one group of people have a right to rule another group of people. So-called Jews and Europeans have exercised this perverted right over other people for centuries. Religion also implies that one group of people are inferior to another group of people. Some religions teach that those who think differently are "dogs, snakes, and devils." The snipers felt that their victims were "justifiable homicides" simply because they lived in America, purchased goods from stores, and gas stations in America; thus their purchases helped to strengthen the economy of the enemy (America). Therefore, their death was symbolic to the killers; it meant the weakening of the American economy through sheer terror. As sick as this line of reasoning may seem to a humane person, you must realize that no crime is done without a distorted form of justification. Every act committed by mankind, whether good or bad, is first justified in the mind. Osama bin Laden believes that "all Americans are targets," and he uses this same line of reasoning.

When the atomic bomb was developed the protagonist felt they were doing the world a great favor. Osama bin Laden also thinks that his cause is just and justified. In his mind anyone that is connected to his enemy is fair game. The snipers convinced themselves that their acts would make the world better in the long run, because society had utterly failed them. The movie entitled "The Matrix" was one of their favorite movies, and they reviewed the movie like it was gold.

In the minds of those who made the Atomic Bomb, this awful invention would prevent war because no one would want to use such a weapon to start the avalanche of world destruction; therefore, the makers of the bomb felt justified too. The bomb would serve as a preventive measure to keep mankind in check, or so they thought. Its use in Japan demonstrated that such a weapon could bring an end to war very fast! Subsequently, the use of the Atomic bomb did not serve its original intent, and Presidents Bush attacking a sovereign nation (Iraq) will not serve its purpose in the long run. In addition, the violence the snipers used will not serve its original objective, it was all in vain.

The masses subconsciously think in the same way: violence can be used to bring an end to a complex situation real fast. This same kind of psychology pervades the ghettoes of America. This is why young people do not hesitate to use violence to settle conflicts, or even scores. Pick up any newspaper and you will read articles depicting the use of violence in the streets of America. It has become a common form of communication between insecure people.

Since World War II violence has been used more by common man to bring resolution to a conflict then any other solution. It must also be noted the slave-holders used all kinds of brutal methods to control those enslaved for centuries with legal protection. In the early 1700's black people could be legally murdered for trying to run away from their so-called Master's.

I contend that those who created the atomic bomb had the same type of mentality as the snipers. President Bush has the same type of mindset, and we should pray to Yahweh that those insecure people in Washington D.C will not advance to the level of pyromaniacs. Laws have always been used to justify brutal acts by governments, and insecurity has always been used by individuals when they act out violently.

I repeat, the slave-codes of Virginia justified the killing of runaways, and the financiers of the Atomic Bomb "legalized" its invention to serve a more diabolical means of promoting and establishing a *New World Order*. Power and control are the motivators that ignite people to use violence in conflict resolution. Until we are willing to see violence for what it really is, it will be used repeatedly during our lifetime, and more so after we perish. Governments will use it, and people on the streets will use it to solve their problems.

The world has been sectionalized through religion, economics, and philosophy. And even in its demarcation the white man is still on top while billions of people suffer poverty and disease. Until we take an honest look at ourselves, as a living entity, as a society that is capable of living in peace; in abundance, and in love with life and others, then violence will be the "god" of the day, or the "doom" of night. We will either live in peace, or die in war. The future will depend on the observance of the present. *What we do with what we see today will determine the course of tomorrow.* If we fail to investigate the events of today, then tomorrow will mirror the mistakes of the past. In spite of the horrendous acts the sniper inflicted on innocent people, we can learn a lot about ourselves in his evil deeds. There lurks a psychology of killing in all of us, and it is evident in the crimes we read about daily in local newspapers.

You may find it indecorous of me to write a book on the "Psychology of Killing," but you will think otherwise upon completion of this eye-opener. In this book you will learn who the real target of the serial snipers was through an anagram that the author will reveal later in the book. There will be a page detailing the significance of the anagram. You will get an idea on how anagrams work and how they can be used to solve "esoteric crimes" in the future. The Federal Bureau of Investigation uses anagrams to solve "signature crimes" when called upon by local authorities. Learning how to decode certain words and phrases will keep you from jumping to premature conjectures when information is relayed to you over the evening news. You must keep in the forefront of your mind the fact that the authorities will not permit certain information to be released before, or after the investigation. The masters in charge think that some information should never fall into the hands of regular citizens. Many things are kept from the masses for obvious reasons. There are things that took place during the sniper investigation that the public will never know, because those that rule the world do not want you to know it, or they feel it will jeopardize classified information. The media might know it, but they dare to share it with you without permission from their masters. I consider the news outlets the voice of the *beastly system* and they will never go against their master's of deceit.

By beastly, the author equates the system with a gluttonous machine that lives off the blood of the land, and uses the people to do all the drudgery of labor. The media is a shield that protects the beast from unwanted criticism, and keeps the people in a state of dizziness. Howard Zinn, author and historian, talks about going outside the "big media" for accurate information. I was very impressed with his interview on C-SPAN, which aired on December 26, 2002. Not very often do you see on television intellectuals with a healthy critique of America's internal organs. I am referring to its cancerous organs that threaten to turn our society into an irradiated wasteland. Amazingly, the same people who claim to be *the light of the world* created a bomb capable of radiating life from the world. Robert Julius Oppenheimer (1904-1967), U.S. nuclear physicist, is accredited with being instrumental in the making of the Atomic bomb. Since that time the Atomic Bomb has developed into a thermo-nuclear bomb that makes the original bomb look like a firecracker.

How can a quasi-Jew be part of manufacturing '*a light*' that produces wholesale death and continue to consider himself a chosen person of *Yahweh*? Go back and re-read the history books and count how many innocent civilians were killed in Japan *(collateral damage)*. Have you heard of a Jew apologizing to the Japanese people for one of their own creating the bomb that killed hundreds of thousands of Japanese civilians? I bet you have not, but they want the entire world to remember and apologize for their holocaust under Nazi Germany. They are too arrogant to offer an apology to the victims of their crimes. Jews were instrumental in bringing African-American slaves to North America, but they do not utter a word of apology, and they never will, because their religion teaches them that they have a right to rule the world. This is a duty they feel Yahweh invested upon them, a chosen people, so to speak.

It is important that we correlate past violence against innocent civilians with current violence against innocent populations, this will enable us to see where the future is headed if we do not correct our ways. Our children learn not only from their lifetime experiences, they also learn from what history teaches to be acceptable under peculiar circumstances, and this information is passed on through the genes. If certain stimuli justifies the extreme use of force in the minds of political leaders then what stops or prevents those on the lower rung of society from feeling justified in the use of brutal force when they feel violated?

John Allen Muhammad participated in the Persian Gulf War that President Bush's father started, so violence was a way of handling non-negotiable disputes to him, or at least that was the way he was previously trained to think. Perhaps, he is a victim of Gulf War Syndrome. "When all else fails kill the bastard," this is how military people must think in order to become a soldier. Conflicts will come and encounters must be resolved.

Even the investigation of the Beltway Sniper evoked confrontation between government agencies. Jim Clemente, the FBI who found the bullet in Fredericksburg, Virginia told the author how sheriffs departments were ill equipped to do a thorough analysis of the crime scene. He stated that there are a lot of at variance over who had "legal jurisdiction." It is hard to look at violence or victims of violence without getting emotional, and this emotionalism came out in jurisdictional battles over who would try the suspects first. I often think about how America was formed and maintained; slaughtering aboriginals, enslaving Africans, and deceptive practices that kept Europeans on top and I see how violent Americans can truly be. The snipers think like Americans, plain and simple. If you think America is not maintained with violence try to shift the power from white people to black people, and you will see how violent white people really are. They will refuse to count your vote, and bring up all your dirty laundry to create an image of you in the public eye that will spell disaster for your public persona. When the authorities got their suspect they wrangled over who would kill the bastards first! Is this civilized or what? The first question should have been do we have the killers? And then let the court system weigh the facts before a dispassionate jury.

## Jurisdictional Feuds

The puppet masters ☫ teach you what they <u>think</u> you should know. What you <u>need</u> to know is completely ignored or kept from you. Even if you disagree with the author's theories surrounding the sniper case I hope you discover how much I love the American people. My criticism of the so-called all-powerful oligarchy should not be mistaken for *anti-Americanism*. Nor should your exaggerated *patriotism* cause you to view me as psychotic for not being equally excited about the world being on the brink of Nuclear Holocaust *(Korea, Iran, and Iraq)* in these last days as President Bush appears to be. To the contrary, I have so much love for the *global community* that I put my reputation on the line in writing this manuscript. My book is a silent protest against evil *in high places,* not the so-called *'Axis of evil'* President Bush talks about. I regret the current debate over whether or not the *Military Industrial Complex* will use Robert Oppenheimer's upgraded toy in their fight to dominant the entire globe. In this book I will write about world events that define and match the snipers 'psychology of killing' on a global scale, while at the same time decode clues about the sniper case that should be considered by free thinkers. Clues, I think, should have been shared with the American people.

From the outset, I do not think the sniper case was handled appropriately by law enforcement and there are things being kept from the general public about the case that I will reveal in this volume. Therefore, I will share some obvious inconsistencies that would make a chicken pluck its feathers and snatch off its own head. I remind you that things are not always as they seem. Many things are happening on the International scene that looks 'isolated' when in fact they are 'orchestrated' by hidden hands and they are 'connected.' You will never know everything about the sniper case because certain forces do not want you to know. However, I promise to disappoint those forces that wish you did not know certain things about this case.

## Closed Doors

There appeared to be an effort to disconcert the investigation by not allowing essential evidence to go across jurisdictional lines. The sniper was aware of these discrepancies among law enforcement and took advantage of the legal power struggle-taking place behind closed doors. This is the reason why the snipers kept going across jurisdictional lines. Subsequently, jurisdictional feuds took place during the middle of the night and the sniper was allowed to catnap right in front of the police, literally. Law enforcement actually spoke with the accused sniper in parking lots right across the street from shootings moments after victims were shot. At one point local police spoke with the sniper in a parking lot of a huge shopping Mall.

Objectivity raced out of the realm of possibility in the sniper case and police were saying anything to the media while overlooking obvious clues. The media helped to further confuse the investigation by focusing on a white vehicle knowing the vehicle was a different color, according to some witnesses. In a large-scale criminal investigation you cannot, I repeat, you cannot become obsessed with one lead, one idea, one vehicle, or one person. In metropolitan terrorist-assault using sniper lines of attack you should never narrow your search down to one car, or one person. I will give you two exceptions that allow the listing of one car in a criminal investigation of such magnitude. You can focus on one car once you are 100% certain of the identity of the suspect, or if you are in hot pursuit of a mobile suspect. Even then you must watch out for second level get-away-cars hidden in alleys or storage facilities. You should never have overhead media Helicopters reporting the roadblocks exact location, allowing the terrorist to take alternative routes, or simply positioning himself in a nearby hotel or storage facility until the heat diminishes.

The snipers would drive a few blocks and just "lay low" while officers frantically stopped every car on the interstate. Common sense should have told the police to check back streets and alleys, not the interstate. Nonetheless, when you have become impatient insanity is not far from you, and you overlook the obvious. You no longer know where reason is and you become unreasonable. You run out and pull over every white van in a ten mile radius, find nothing, and start the frenzy all over again with no positive results. At some point you should realize that another car may also be involved, or that the white van may be a signal to shoot. You know, "when you see a white van let me know, since initial reports said something about a white van." Authorities should have kept the white van a secret, because mentioning a white van made the public see nothing but white vans. The nation was under the spell of faulty reporting and wild imaginings which were promoted on every news station. In the end, the car was obviously not a white van.

## The Investigative Project

Stephen Denny, a member of "The Investigative Project" that was set up after the terrorist attacks of 911 said prematurely that the sniper assault is likely the work of a sporadic killer "who makes up targets as he goes along." Nothing could have been further from the truth. He said that this kind of killer is hard to catch. But, in fact, they caught him ten times and let him go. He was let go several times in spite of a warrant for his arrest on the books in Tacoma, Washington for shoplifting and not appearing in court last March. Mr. Denny does not believe the suspects are part of a convoluted cell. But the suspect allegedly ran an elaborate smuggling operation from the Caribbean Islands, planned the kidnapping of the Antigua Prime Minister Lester Bird, and sought explosives to rob banks, and manufactured sophisticated passports with high tech-equipment, even talked openly to his associates about blowing up tankers on interstate highways. To do all this suspect had to have some connections. For Mr. Denny to make this type of statement without a thorough investigation is ludicrous when you consider the scope of the crimes the suspects are being accused of. How did investigators forget that Richard Reid- the Antigua-ticketed "shoe bomber" convicted of trying to blow up a trans-Atlantic airplane chose the same Island for destructive purposes? More than one coincidence could equate to one massive orchestra of deliberate conspiracies. Everyone in the band does not have to know each other to play the same music.  All you would need to know is how to read musical notes and you can play with the band. Who wrote the notes for John Allen Muhammad?

One of the most known things about "terrorist cells" is that it is best that members not know each other. The less one knows about other players, the more capable the organization of terror can operate. If one cell gets caught they cannot report what they do not know. It is foolish to think terrorist act alone. These types of "units" share information on a "need to know" basis.

### Alfred P. Murrah

In cases like this you cannot underestimate conspiracy, nor can you rush to judgment. You would think local law enforcement and the Federal Bureau of Investigation would know better, especially after the bombing of the Alfred P. Murrah Building in Oklahoma City. As a concerned citizen, I find it strange that everything Mark Koernke, a former U.S. Army intelligence officer and Counter-intelligence Analyst predicted about the New World Order, ♟ is unfolding just like he described in his cheep home videos, which I have viewed several times over the last 10 years. Although I do not agree with much of Mr. Koernke's estimation of resolution when it comes to the "race problem," I do think he is correct in his analysis of the New World Order ♟. United States Supreme Justice Louis Brandeis once said, "A little Sunlight is the best disinfectant," meaning an independent press is the best way in which to keep government pure and honest. As much as ignorant people seem to dislike critics like Steve Cokely, Mark Koernke, Louis Farrakhan, and William Cooper, we need them to inform us on the hidden agendas that affect our lives. William Cooper can no longer share his insights into the New World Order because a sheriff's deputy shot him to death while allegedly serving a warrant at midnight in Arizona.

## Material Witness

You may remember that Mr. Koernke was briefly detained for questioning after the *Oklahoma City Bombing* for allegedly having ties to Timothy McVeigh. However, in my recollection the public was never thoroughly informed about the outcome of the initial investigation that involved Mr. Koernke. Strangely enough, Mark Koernke, like Nathaniel Osborne, was questioned in Michigan and let go. No crime was placed on either so-called "material witness." Association with the main culprit apparently was their only crime. It is a dangerous precedence to detain someone as a "material witness," but never publicize the results in high profile cases that affect the entire population. If a person is found innocent in these high profile cases, the media should be just as excited in reporting that outcome to its listeners as it was about the initial arrest. There needs to be a committee from the grassroots who can watch what "big brother" is doing, a people's committee to make sure our rights are not violated during the wee hours of the night and we get shot between the eyes like William Cooper, the author of *'Behold a Pale Horse.'* Some kind of procedure that protects our rights, besides courtrooms ran by Masonic Judges and special interest groups. Secret societies should not be running our lives, sitting on court benches, or forming new laws while bedecked in black gothic robes. If you and I continue to sit back doing nothing they will be rushing us to the "gas chamber." I have had so many friends express fear about me writing this speculative book. What does that tell you about the realization of freedom in North America? Citizens are afraid to take a closer look at their own government. Common sense will tell you to pay close attention to the most powerful government the world has ever seen. I do not agree with Timothy McVeigh's way of handling suspicion, so I write books instead.

Those who are familiar with the Timothy McVeigh and Terry Lynn Nichols case will remember that the mysterious John Doe number 2 was never caught. McVeigh took some crucial information with him to the grave, never revealing the true global connection of his misdeed. I am willing to bet that his co-conspirators are still out there, lurking, waiting, plotting, and planning the next man-made catastrophe. Mr. McVeigh's skull and bones ☠ would quiver from the grave and come back to life if the truth got out. I hope that the sniper will share his global connection, if there is one, before the "ultimate penalty is prescribed," so that the people can plan to protect themselves from the invisible hand of butchery in the future. Perhaps, Terry Lynn Nichols will give us the answers we need.

On another note there really needs to be an investigation on why so many Gulf War veterans are killing their wives after their tour of duty (this is a reference to the Fort Bragg Murders) and developing anti-American sentiments. The media reported that John Allen Muhammad suffered from the disease of Anti-Americanism. I hope this is not a situation to set up and quarantine anyone who intellectually opposes certain political and philosophical perspectives in the Bush Doctrine. To question a philosophical idea, like the New World Order, does not make one Anti-American, and people should not be afraid to debate politics publicly through literature and speech. Since 911 conscious writers seem to be silenced into oblivion.

As a citizen I am really alarmed about the vaccinations veterans received to ward off biological warfare in Iraq years ago. Is it possible the vaccine is having adverse effects on their amygdale gland and the military is keeping it a secret? If "Accutane" can come under investigation for possibly causing teen-agers to commit suicide, become psychotic, or abort their fetuses, then maybe certain specified injections from the military should be monitored for possibly influencing homicidal fantasies. I can see the logic in wanting soldiers to become homicidal maniacs. The *Military Industrial Complex* would not want to produce a choirboy that specialized in throwing pink flowers at the enemy; they want someone capable of killing. War is about winning and winning is negotiated through mass killings. A flower thrower would literally be considered a *soft target, no pun intended.*

I find it very disturbing that a person can be considered, or labeled anti-American for having an opposing view on the interpretation of crime! I find it extremely disgusting for someone to kill another just because they think different or look different. I do not fear what the evil empire can do to me for writing this book, but I do understand the danger. As I said above, a sheriff's deputy in Arizona murdered William Cooper at midnight after Cooper wrote dozens of books, articles, and essays on the New World Order and President Bush's connection to Skull and Bones. Sometimes the penalty for having a brain of your own is death. You are to live in America, not question what you see here! I will not apologize for questioning notorious events that affect us all in some way. With that said, let us now consider the 3rd person in the *Oklahoma Bombing* case.

## Third Party

Who was John Doe number 2? What ever happened to the $2 million reward that was put on his head? Isn't it strange that he looked just like Jose Padilla, the so-called suspect of the dirty bomb scare who was arrested years later? Two gulf war veterans and a mystery man in the *Oklahoma City* case. Conspiracy theorist may be seeing some marked characteristics and similarities in the sniper case. Some conscious people watching the sniper case think there were three suspects in the parking lot where the lady was killed in Alabama, allegedly by the sniper suspects on September 21, 2002. If one suspect was holding the 223-caliber rifle and the other suspect allegedly left his fingerprint at the crime scene as well as a .22-calber pistol, then who drove the get-away car the police talked about? If fingerprints was left at the crime scene at the liquor store what kept law enforcement from rigorously trying to identify a suspect to arrest?

## National Crime Information Center

Would you have me to believe that the fingerprints were never placed in the National Crime Information Center database for a widely divergent search? American people should demand more professionalism from those charged to protect our vital interest. Could there have been a third party at the crime scene in Alabama? If so, will he get caught years later plotting to produce organized chaos? Law enforcement is keeping life-saving information from the American people. The secret government ☥ has advised them that to do so is in the best interest of National Security. Consequently, crimes are not being properly investigated, especially if the crimes help to usher in a New World Order.

## Satellite Surveillance

From the outset, I would like to suggest that the government knew the identity of the sniper through tips, satellite surveillance, focal triangulation, warnings, and exact descriptions of the automobile from the very beginning, and yet, John was never considered a suspect by law enforcement. Why not? And who should be responsible for answering this question? Did it have anything to do with the separation of Military and State? You may find it puzzling that the suspect was captured sneaking illegal immigrants into the country and was quickly let go. At his arraignment in Florida it was noted that he had over 22 false identifications on him. (If you have time rent the movie entitled "Borne Identity," and it will show you why professional assassins have multiple identities). Not to mention the two illegal immigrants that stood by his side, one being the younger suspect's mother. Normally, I would not find that too surprising, but post-911 I would find it shocking! You want me to believe that a Muslim is caught after the terrorist attacks of 911 sneaking illegal immigrants into the country, in Florida, at an airport, the same state where the hijackers took up flying lessons, and no one does anything about it?

## Regional Jurisdiction

The Federal Bureau of Investigation was not notified, and if they were notified, where is the file specifying how the situation should be handled, or stating how the situation was handled? I find this to be very suspicious post-911. If this blunder is true, who will be responsible for the negligence of poor insight by our government? I am not the smartest person in the world to see that Florida is a point of entry for international terrorist. Nor am I so imbecilic to recognize that President Bush's brother is governor of that regional jurisdiction ☠. If John Allen Muhammad played a key role in helping to smuggle illegal immigrants into this monolithic nation, how can you reduce him to a petty criminal who became enraged over a failed marriage? No, this sniper case appears to be bigger than that! Red flags are popping up everywhere! The common person on the street cannot see what is going on because of their supernatural faith in the American system. How many people know what was allegedly found in the snipers alleged killing machine (Car)?

- Laptop Computer
- Global Positioning System
- Walkie-talkies
- Fake Identifications
- Bushmaster XM-15 Rifle
- 223-Caliber Bullets
- One Glove
- Bi-pod
- High Powered Scope
- Notebook with pin
- Map of Metropolitan area
- Dietary Book (How to eat to live, By Elijah Muhammad)
- Esoteric Literature
- Clothing
- Tape

## Classified Information

A Global Positioning System (GPS) device was found in the accused radar-protected automobile. Aerospace Corporation in El Segundo, California works directly with the United States Military and they know how close Americans are being watched daily. Classified information on citizens worldwide is transferred from El Segundo to the Pentagon daily. Have you noticed the car is painted dark like the Stealth Bomber? A dark car is difficult to see on radar at night from space. John Allen Muhammad would know this from his military training at Fort Lewis. Fort Lewis is famous for its comprehensive "special agent training" and "elite sniper unit." Was the car purchased dark, or was it painted that color with a special paint? What was the color of the car before the car dealer at *'Sure Shot Auto shop in Camden'* purchased it? There are several ways a car can be detected using modern technology. I find it very strange that *the car belonged to law enforcement* before being sold to *Sure Shot Auto Shop*. How long was the car at *Sure Shot Auto Shop* before being purchased by John Allen Muhammad? Did John get instructions from *an elite assassins* group to purchase the car from 'Sure Shot' to complete a special assignment? *It simply troubles my mind that the sniper would be driving an undercover police car that was previously used in specific undercover operations.* I wonder if the same rigged up engine was left in the car for quick escape. You know police cars have high performance engines that can outrun ordinary cars. More than one co-incidence makes a twist of fate seem deliberate. I believe the Chevy Caprice was designed purposely to circumvent radar from space. You remember the Bat-Mobile was dark too. Batman and his younger partner got their assignments from a rich commissioner ☻ who lived underground in a secret hide away. We know that John is older than Malvo, but we do not know who commissioned them to kill innocent people.

## Cloverleaf Contours

The thermo-energy emanating from the engine is hard to detect from under a tree, because a tree is a living organism that emits more heat at night. That is the possible reason the sniper laid low at rest stops, concealing his vehicle under trees. But why did he use highways that were shaped like a flower (cloverleaf contours) for fast escape?

In an urban area heat tracing from space is very difficult to monitor at crowded intersections because multiple heat-emitting vehicles crisscross at traffic circles. This was the main reason for using escape routes where entry to the interstate was shaped like a cloverleaf. Satellites have a hard time locating mobile heat because heat curls in an upward motion and then spreads before dissolving. From space it looks like bubbles that pop before disappearing. Heat from automobiles crisscross at intersections and appear to tangle together when seen from space. I think this kind of entanglement makes it hard to detect mobile heat from space as the sun crosses the horizon.

## Concealment

Also urban areas produce multiple heat discharging devices. Assassins learn these things when training for urban operations. I'm sure that the sniper read Mark V. Lonsdale's book, "Sniper Counter Sniper: a guide for special response teams." Professional snipers learn about tactical communications, range estimation, concealment, computing trajectory, accuracy, guerrilla warfare, scouting, and disciplinary proficiency that produce the mind-set for completing a task. Army Major Willis Powell improved sniper training in 1968. They learn to simultaneously hit their target while preparing to move to a neutral area out of harms way. Concealment is a critical part of surprise assault in performance conditioning. A good sniper, if there is such a thing, camouflages in the natural surroundings. If he uses a car the highway would be the best place to hide or blend in. A professional sniper would know this. He aims to hit his target and escape without being detected.

## Triangulation

There are ways to confuse visibility from space. Triangulation is hard to track when you have multiple heat sources. However, the GPS device is in constant contact with satellites, sending signals periodically from the laptop computer and GPS, showing the exact location frequented by the vehicle, how long it was there, speeds in route and the time the car left the location. Even when the GPS is turned off it still sends signals periodically. Triangulation methods are used to pinpoint exact locations of GPS devises. Therefore, the Pentagon monitored the car from space the whole time the GPS system was in the car. It would be interesting to know how long the GPS device was in the car and where it was purchased? The media reported that a shooting victim in Maryland had his GPS system stolen from him by the sniper, if that is the case police should have hunted down the GPS system from the start. Satellite companies were hijacked of copies of recorded imagery from GPS devices in northern Virginia using scrambling devices at the Pentagon during the sniper investigation. A secret team was assigned to intercept sporadic GPS movement. Apparently none of this information was given to law enforcement.

GPS devices were probably used to get the ex-act coordinates of the World Trade Center too back in 2001. Your average criminal would know nothing about GPS systems or how Big Brother monitors them daily. The U.S Department of Transportation was alerted to monitor any sporadic driving near and around the Washington D.C. area. Several video recordings were sent to Law enforcement, but overlooked and brushed aside. They even sent a tape of the Chevy Caprice going through a red light during the so-called investigation of the sniper case. In spite of the video surveillance being relayed to the police, they get you to focus on a white Chevy Astro with a ladder on top. They got us thinking white is black and black is white. I do not know what kind of magic this is, but I distrust the smell of it. When the smoke clears we may have more answers, or we may find ourselves with a bad cold.

## Microchip Technology

Again, a signal is sent automatically to the satellite even when the GPS system is turned off. Microchip technology is a science that common people underestimate or simply have no knowledge of. If you knew how closely we are being watched it would cause you to become extremely paranoid if your mind is weak. That same microchip will be placed under your skin in the near future under the pretext of small pox vaccinations. It will also be in your driver's license real soon, sooner than you think.

A little girl voluntarily received the microchip earlier this year when several girls came up dead after being abducted from their homes. It is so small that it can enter your skin by way of a hypodermic needle. Veterinarians are already using this device on animals. If you have some understanding of the nature of the enemy you may gather enough common sense to fight him off and survive his bedevilment with wisdom. I think that John Allen Muhammad was controlled by a microchip.

I assure you that Americans have no privacy rights anymore. Call your local congressman and ask for all the data on "Total Information Awareness." You will be shocked! Somewhere in the Pentagon each shooting has been secretly taped and digitized under a special code. No, I am not insane. Unlike many Americans, I have erased *fear* from my mind and I pay close attention to what is not being said on the evening news. You are so spellbound by what the media tells you, that the obvious escapes your mental responsiveness. Yes, you have been lulled to sleep. You are a victim of psychological warfare; which means, you have been conditioned to believe everything you see on major networks, but you automatically doubt anything coming from so-called uncultivated people like myself. Subconsciously, you are terrified of *big brother*! (I suggest that you read George Orwell's books: Animal Farm and 1984).

## Media Control

Once you escape from *"media control"* you may think or suspect that the government is holding essential information from you, especially after reading this brief report. If you are really asleep you may write me off as some crazed lunatic or super paranoid individual. I really do not care what you think about me, but I will share the outcome of my own impecunious investigation with the general public through this paperback book. I have spent over $10,000 doing this research and it was worth it. I am aware that some of this information is speculative and cannot be proven. Hopefully, it will give you something to think about. I will write about things your local papers are forbidden to mention. Industrial interest groups control most newspapers and they are obliged to stay on the line and inside the center ☠. They are only allowed to target specific details in controversal stories. Reporters automatically know how far *right* or how far *left* to cover a particular story. Journalists are taught what is acceptable reporting and what is not. I am a self-educated man with a brain of my own, and I am coming to you live from the grassroots section of society. We do not need your permission to write about anything. I am free! But supervisors who represent special interest groups imprison writers with big journalistic names. Small guys like me have nothing to lose, but our chains. I write books with my chains as I attempt to escape mediocrity.

For instance, your local newspapers reported that the killer left clues right along his path of death. Have you noticed they have not tried to decipher those clues? They know that certain information must be ignored because its revelation will shatter the mythology of the *lone sniper theory*. In *high profile assassinations* reporters are quick to paint a picture of some angry killer acting alone. They are hesitant to look into the possibility of an intricate network of co-conspirators working in collaboration with secret societies ☠ to promote a New World Order ☠.

The world is still waiting to see the secret reports on the November 22, 1963 assassination of President Kennedy. In the sniper case these co-conspirators could include informants, arms suppliers, training facilities, associates, financiers, and secret agents who get orders from higher-ups. Everyone must be suspect in high profile assassinations. I believe the sniper case is one of those high profile assassinations that demand further investigation. American people should be especially careful before reaching a conclusive opinion when black leaders are killed since minorities have no way of determining hidden motives that would drive one to kill a member of their rank. Four of Malcolm X's killers were never caught, even though the New York Police department knew their names in 1965.

I want to know why Kenneth H. Bridges was killed by the snipers. This does not underscore the tragedy of the other victims in the sniper case. It would take further research to determine what role they may have had in the snipers mind. I do not know if they were random victims necessarily, or if the sniper was given specific orders from some elite assassins group. We simply do not know enough at this time to outright discharge that possibility. It would take a team working full-time to solve that riddle. You would have to study the street names, buildings, and the functions of each individual in this complex matrix of human affairs. I automatically have some suspicion about the FBI analyst that was victimized, but I do not have the resources or time to look into it. I wonder if she had anything to do with the initial investigation. I do know that she was "terminally ill." Perhaps, she was about to reveal some inside information on the sniper case. That would be something to investigate. You never know who is calling the shots.

## Kennedy Papers

Intelligent people should ask why bureaucratic procedure did not allow pertinent information that the sniper left behind to be shared amongst different agencies. If different agencies are denied pertinent information, what do you think they are keeping from you? Will the truth be sealed for twenty-five years like the Kennedy papers? Will there be a congressional inquiry into the sniper case after the suspects are executed? The sniper investigation was just as sloppy as the Kennedy examination thirty-nine years ago. Sloppiness in the sniper case would translate into vital information being overlooked, brushed aside, or not considered at all by other jurisdictional bureaus, and this would equate to the sniper having more time to exterminate unsuspecting people.

## Triangulation Crossfire

Shortly after the presidential assassination on that dark Friday in 1963, the *triangulation crossfire* was overlooked and never thoroughly scrutinized. A White Chevy 4-door car was seen driving from the scene that was completely ignored. Witnesses crucial to the investigation came up dead and some were detained in mental wards indefinitely.

Secret societies will go to any length to win the war on deception, even if it means coups, propaganda, psyche-warfare, and rigged elections; none of these methodologies should be neglected, according to Special Agents Reports that leaked to the masses.

J. Edgar Hoover wrote a book entitled "Masters of Deceit." You do not have to go far back in time to see the skullduggery ✗

of the previous Bush Administration, the FBI, or of the Central Intelligence Agency. Yale graduates have played a pivotal role in the CIA and this is public information. This powerful family (The Bush's) took the presidential nomination from Al Gore as a result of the deliberate miscount in Florida. George Bush's father, a previous president and member of Skull and Bones ♟ allowed Reagan to use the military to sale drugs in South America, and yet, he was never impeached, nor was President Reagan impeached. You remember the Iran-Contra Affair. Oliver North and John Poindexter were forced to take the weight in that case. Now John Poindexter, according to Al Gore, is in charge of collecting all information on American people at the pentagon.

## International Terrorism

Did the administration allow the killings in the sniper case to continue in order to build support for its Homeland Security Act, or its invasion into Iraq? This could only be possible if the *secret military* ♟ knew the identity of the sniper. *Black operations* keep the Whitehouse ashen and Europe in safe hands. Is the truth stored at some classified location waiting for the public to discover it once this generation dies off? You know, keep the public thinking that the sniper case may be connected with *international terrorism, or some lone mad-man acting out over a family separation* and the people will demand that their own civil rights be put aside in order to protect them from Osama Ben Laden, or crazed mad-man like Saddam, and other uncertain terrorist networks. Our newfound patriotism will not allow us to look at the role our own government may have played in the sniper case or any other terrorist act. I am referring to our *racist foreign policy* that allows children to starve to death in Africa. It is not important that we solve these matters in this lifetime, some may say. Wait until the guilty get old and evaporate. Then tell the people the truth on how they have been conditioned to self-destruct or how our government manipulated world affairs to cause us to reach this cataclysmic stage. This could be interpretive of secret operations taking place in the military or information being kept from us relating to pharmacology and germ warfare. It is now common knowledge that the military requires some of its personal to use stimulants to fight fatigue. This government will win "by any means necessary."

## After the Guilty Die

After the guilty die you can tell the people how certain drugs created psychopathic disorders or how the military wanted to start wars for strategic purposes. I often wonder if the chaos is designed to bring about a scientific order, a controlled chaos, and a global administration. Human beings are not supposed to be harming each other at the rate they are doing today. Is something in the food? What has gone wrong with our world? Is it in the drugs, this maladjusted behavior is not normal?

## Tarot

Is it possible that a secret organization *Trains Assassins Rigorously Over Time* (T.A.R.O.T) and place certain individuals from the Tarot Team on special assignments to promote hidden agendas? I am aware that this sounds ridiculous, but before you think this impossible go back and look at the movie JFK and EXECITIVE ORDER. When citizens cannot speculate on what government may or may not be doing, you know that "democracy is nothing but hypocrisy," like Malcolm X, the dyed in the wool revolutionary, stated before he was assassinated. I repeat, I write this short book without any fear or caution. Fear is the main component to justify a Fascist State ☠. Yes, the sniper case guaranteed the passage of the Homeland Security Act, a neo-Fascist State, because of the fear it produced. As far fetched as this may sound, I would love to hear some of the conversation that was going on in the White House back in October 2002. Some politicians thought the sniper case was the fuel they needed to pass the Homeland Security Act and they shared this concept amongst themselves. Your average American has no clue what the Homeland Security Act means to their individual freedom, nor can they see how the *Constitution* has been legally suspended post-911.

## The Enabling Act

The Homeland Security Act can only be compared to Adolf Hitler's Enabling Act of March 23, 1933. The Enabling Act promised to "deviate from the constitution" while keeping the "powers of the President intact." Common people will never consider such diabolical schemes by a government ran by Skull and Bones ☠! I suggest you read "The Biggest Secret" by David Icke for a more comprehensive explanation of Skull and Bones ☠. Also read, "Behold the Pale Horse," by the recently murdered William Cooper. Their books will also help you understand how governments take advantage of crisis events (Ordo Ab Chao). You may want to read "Secret of The Tomb" by Alexandra Robbins as well. She gives detailed information on the secret society called "Skull and Bones" at Yale University. The sniper ordeal was great for political promoters of less privacy laws and ultra surveillance apparatus. I repeat, Al Gore says that the Bush Administration has placed Admiral John Poindexter over the "Total Information Awareness" unit at the pentagon. This is allegedly the same Admiral John Poindexter who was caught up in the Iran-Contra scandal during the Reagan Administration. Everyone who has loyalties to Skull and Bones ☠ are being maneuvered into strategic positions to set up the Permanent Government. The Enabling Act created a new order for Germany and unified all centralized intelligence. Homeland Security will, or should I say, is doing the same thing for Bush's Administration. The price of your safety is now directly related to your lose of freedom. In order to be safe, you must now pay for it with the destruction of your individual freedom. With all the budget cuts in Virginia, the sniper case allowed the governor to save resources for the Department of Public Health and Safety. Before the sniper case there was to be a significant reduction in federal dollars for public safety. I wonder if this is one of the reasons the sniper was allowed to go about his business of killing without being identified.

I suspect that the Police knew the killer was a black person mid-way through the serial killings but decided not to inform the public. Why Not?

## False Information

On September 14, 2002 witnesses saw the Chevy Caprice, driving from the Beer and Wine Store where a 22 year old man was critically wounded from a rifle bullet. This same description was given to police several times, near and around shooting scenes. How can a car be at multiple shooting scenes and escape the attention of law enforcement? You do not have to be a rocket scientist to realize that the description should have been given to the American people long ago. I find it unethical that the description of the car was kept from the public. Ten people would be alive today if the information was relayed to the masses in a responsible way.

## All Points Bulletin

At some stage the Metropolitan Police Department put out an
_All Points Bulletin_, which read:

---

**Metropolitan Police Department Report**
**Washington D.C. Jurisdiction**

**LOOK OUT FOR VEHICLE**
Older Model Chevrolet Caprice
Or Vehicle of Similar Style,
Burgundy colored, 4-Door
With Dark tinted Windows

---

Obvious incompetent Investigation on the part of D.C.,
police allowed this oversight to take place. The question
remains unanswered; were the police told to overlook this
piece of evidence from higher up?

In spite of this specific description from a credible witness,
the car was not announced on television. Someone gave the
Montgomery County Police Chief false information about
the Chevy Caprice being set ablaze or abandoned. They told
him not to focus on that specific car. It was hard to decipher that information because the report seemed somewhat
sketchy. The person who relayed that information to Chief
Moose should be questioned at length. I noticed that Chief
Moose never gave his unreliable sources name to local television newscasters.

Even if the car had been set on fire or abandoned wouldn't
it have to be taken to a lab for forensic test? I would think so,
especially if the car was thought to be involved in the sniper
spree. Isn't it obvious to you that the car was ignored by law

enforcement by an order from way up in the ranks? In any homicidal legal action the evidence is gathered and taken to a laboratory for examination. Even if the car was burned beyond recognition it should have been further examined. The fact is there was no burnt car or abandoned vehicle to take anywhere. The Chevy Caprice was stopped ten times during the sniper investigation and the license plate was put through a national police database. Even though the car was listed on police documents as suspect, nothing was found and the killer was allowed to do more damage to the American psyche. I wonder if the Metropolitan Police Department shared their information with other jurisdictions. I am amazed how Chief Moose robotically dodged any questions pertaining to the APB report concerning the Chevy. Go back and look at the footage where reporters questioned Chief Moose about the car. He was visibly shaken. I think it was on October 15, 2002.

## Chief Charles Moose

Chief Charles Moose would only obey that kind of order if it came from the top. No small time cop or detective could make Chief Moose accept the outcome of the burnt vehicle or abandoned car theory. I suspect that the Chevy Caprice was talked about immediately after the Department of Transportation sent the FBI footage showing the vehicle running a red light near a shooting scene or receiving its description on September 14, 2002 in the Silver Springs, Maryland attack. Amazingly the car was stopped almost a dozen times during the esoteric killing spree! Yes, police caught Muhammad running a red light on October 20, 2002 and let him go. This was a day before the Bus Driver was murdered. I have proven that Higher-ranking members of law enforcement knew of this car long before that minor traffic violation. Mathematically speaking, the chances of a car being stopped ten times in three weeks should have raised eye-brawls. If they were not aware of it why would they be giving Chief Moose information about it? You cannot discuss with somebody something you are not aware of, that would be an empty conversation.

## Death Machine

The sniper suspect was briefly detained in Baltimore during the sniper investigation for sleeping in the same Vehicle on the evening of October 7, 2002? This was after the initial report describing the Chevy Caprice as a possible snipers nest and death machine. Again, he was let go. A man told the police that a person was shooting from the boot of a 1990 Chevy Caprice and gave a thorough description of the driver. A woman gave the exact description of a dark Caprice driving from the shooting too. Both saw the same car at the same time. Two black witnesses that were completely overlooked during the sniper investigation did not get credit for helping to solve the riddle. The man gave them enough information for an "arrest and a conviction." You tell me what in the hell is going on? All of his information was overlooked. Why and how did the White Van become the focal point of the investigation? It would be satisfying to find out who gave Chief Moose the order to move beyond the Chevy Caprice and to concentrate on the white van.

The *reason* for poor follow-up should not be handled lightly, especially in this case. That *reason* may shed light on key people involved in the investigation. You never know who is working on the inside to hamper the investigation for political purposes. *I am not suggesting that the insider is working in cahoots with the criminal, but he may use an incident like the sniper case to lobby for the removal of civil liberties or as an opportune moment to pass restraining policy. In a fascist state random criminality is the fuel to ignite the passage of restric-*

_tive laws_. Hitler used the arson of a government building to remove the people's civil liberties. Will the Bush Administration use "terrorism" to suspend civil liberties?

## Jurisdictional Fighting

Perhaps the lack of follow up was just an oversight. I do not know, but it looks kind of strange to me. We understand that "Jurisdictional fighting always takes place in high profile cases that go across State lines." But that does not justify "The description of the Chevy Caprice" never being shared across jurisdictions or released to the public. This same car was spotted driving away from a Home-Depot store where a person was shot, the lights on the car was cut off. Nonetheless, the public was kept in the dark about it. Sometimes news reporters accidentally drop or leak vital information for the public to peruse. A family member of an officer working the case leaked out the revelation of the Tarot card left at the school. In other words, if they had not leaked that information you and I would not have received it. However, they forgot to report that the common person has no time to study; they are too busy trying to eke out a living. And those who can do simple research are too busy paying back college loans to incompetent institutions that did not teach them anything about governmental analysis, or thorough criminal investigation. Your average onlooker cannot see every report that comes across the evening news; they are picking up kids from the daycare, going to a second job, or resting after getting off the first job that pays the minimum wage. This is why they foolishly trust law enforcement to relay vital information to them in a case like the snipers. Police could lose all creditability if the public thought they withheld vital information from them. Once I saw the _Tarot Card_ I went to work trying to figure out what it meant. My main focus stayed on Benjamin Tasker Middle

School, the location where the *Tarot Card* was left. I also felt that the date of the school shooting was essential to finding out the true extent and meaning of the crimes.

## White Astro Van

Law enforcement must learn to share vital information with the public without jeopardizing the investigation. You cannot blame people for being suspicious of your agency when they learn that you knew the description of the car long ago and failed to report it to the society that was being victimized. No one knew the identity of the snipers. There was absolutely no evidence on who the killer was, or what he wanted, according to law enforcement. A true description of the vehicle would have been much help and could have saved lives.

I repeat, at one shooting scene, October 3, 2002 a black man and a black woman with foreign intonations told the police of a 1990 Chevrolet Caprice that looked suspicious. This was at a crime scene and the information was passed on in a report to police on a Teletype, but it was not given priority. The man even considered the possibility of the shooting being conducted from inside the car, not outside. Again, his input was disregarded. In time it was overlooked.

One reason his claim was ignored was based on his description of the driver as a black man. See, the police developed a strong tunnel vision, which precluded them from seeing black men as serial killers. Objective investigation was obsolete, everybody focused on a white man in a white van. The concerned citizen was obviously not considered a credible witness. The narrow-mindedness of investigative textbooks prevented law enforcement from looking outside the box. Forensic psychologist went on a guessing spree that killed many possibilities.

## Ralph Ellison

What does this reveal about law enforcement when it comes to the black man's voice? Historically, black men in the United States have been ignored by law enforcement. The system has an innate suspicion of the black voice and of the black man in general. Ralph Ellison, the famous author, wrote about how inconsequential the black man is to white America. The black male is not only overlooked for his honorable qualities; he is even disregarded when he is functioning in his worse state of mind. He is simply ignored in America. There seems to be nothing he can do to change his position among racists ☠.

I find it exceedingly disturbing that law enforcement knew that the white van was a distraction or *red herring* from the very beginning of the investigation, but never informed the general public or other locales. Knowing that there are thousands of white vans on American roads produced a severe psychological disturbance in the general population. The level of fear escalated beyond that produced shortly after 911. All white vans became suspect. Families were calling hotlines on their own members reporting their suspicions. Whoever drove a white van was feared up and down the East Coast. I hope this *psyche campaign* was not a precursor or forerunner to sub-consciously make the American people fear the United Nations, who also drive white vehicles, in the future. The serial killer in Baton Rouge, Louisiana is purportedly using a white truck too. I know it is merely coincidental that John Allen Muhammad was born in Baton Rouge, Louisiana. At the publishing of this book a serial killer is accused of killing four women in that State (he has not been caught as of January 4, 2003). One reporter called his vehicle "The Mysterious White Truck." Scripture talks about a pale horse transporting death.

ERIC PENN

## Freedom of Speech

Psychologically, Americans will begin to fear all white vehicles. Remember; when citizens cannot question these possibilities you will already be enslaved. My book will test whether or not we still have *"freedom of speech."* If the government detains me, or harasses me for putting forth these possibilities I will ask for your support. My freedom is just as vulnerable as yours. As a writer my rights should be protected under the United States Constitution. *This book in no way determines the guilt or innocence of John Allen Muhammad. It is merely a poor man's exegesis of the "Psychology of Killing" in America. Law must consider Mr. Muhammad innocent until proven guilty. The theories and concepts put forth are speculative and meant merely to be "thought provoking."*

Education is supposed to allow the student to be creative. I am hoping that you will consider this book an educational and creative tool in forensic science from the grassroots level. Common men also have theories on the motivation of crime, and it would be a crime to deny common men the avenue by which to express those findings. *The people without consequence must police governments if democracy is to be sustained.* On the grassroots level we have no laboratory to dispense judgment; therefore, we use anagrams to get to the root of the problems plaguing our communities.

## Triangular Slave Trade

Whoever was doing the killing would leave a trail of blood in the shape of the *triangular slave trade*. If you take two complete triangles, one in the normal position and the other inverted, you will have a six- pointed star (called Solomon's seal ✡). Remove the horizontal lines from Solomon's seal and you will have left the square and the compass of Freemasonry.

For a more thorough elucidation of Solomon's seal I suggest you read "Born in Blood: The Lost Secrets of Freemasonry" by John J. Robinson. Was the sniper trying to teach the world about a worldwide *Jewish Conspiracy* that threatens to destroy the world thirteen times over in his use of the geographical triangle? Killing people to teach a lesson to the world makes the murderer an animal that is unworthy of respect, dignity, and freedom.

## Esoteric Meaning

Many people do fear that the quasi-Jews are plotting against them. I know people who refuse to take lightly the triangular shaped killing spree and they think it has esoteric meaning in the sniper case! The triangle is seen in the outer peripheral of the killing; on the inside of the triangle you see the shape of a five-pointed star. A triangle is also the shape of the symbol for the *Trilateral Commission*, meaning resurrection, or a coming forth from the dead. The 13th Tarot card has a similar meaning of renewal, change, and transformation. The *Trilateral Commission* understands the significance of symbols. David Rockefeller, a quasi-Jew was the principal founder of the commission. David Rockefeller also owned the land that the United Nations is built on. It is believed that the Rockefeller family owns Exxon gas stations. The snipers only communicated from Exxon gas stations (located at Parham Road and Broad Street) and Kenneth H. Bridges was murdered at an Exxon station. According to the Greek word for *Exxon*, it means they have *the right to* rule. Another quasi-Jew Dr. Zbigniew Brzezinski also played an important role in the formation of the *Trilateral Commission*. Former President George Bush and Alan Greenspan have ties to the same commission. They are all so-called elite members of secret societies, the Ivy League crew. Each one holds a secret key that could build the moral of African American youth, adults, and seniors. Another definition of the triangle is "fire." The fire triangle means that someone is angry. In Christianity you know who lives in the fire (Satan)! Those who hold the secret have a tendency to get angry when the truth leaks out to the general public.

Yale University has a connection to the Jewish people through its founder Elihu Yale. Look at the Hebrew writing on its University seal, it says "Light and Truth." What is it about "Light and Truth" that adorns their University seal? Could it mean to keep the original people from the "light that protects the truth, or the truth that radiates from the light?"

## Jewish Kabala

All of the above people mentioned as *Trilateral Commission* officers have studied the Jewish Kabala and have eternal membership to the Grand Lodge of England. The Queen of England has secretly knighted some or all members of Skull and Bones ☠. They are aware of the urgency to completely overtake the world in a few more years and place a *false messiah* over the people in order to usher in a *British Utopia*. *British* mean "people of the covenant," in Hebrew. September 11, 2001 was used to bring Russia and America together as a single unit. All of this was orchestrated by the British Empire through *The Octopus*. The *false messiah* will look very peaceful in 2004. France is currently working on a new constitution for the European Union. A few American professors are secretly helping the former French President put it together. Skull and Bones ☠ pays homage to the so-called royal family of England who are acting like the *chosen people of the covenant* until the New Jerusalem can be built.

## Significance of Tasker Family

I make mention of all these people so you will know the significance of Benjamin Tasker's Middle School. Benjamin
Tasker's family belonged to the Maryland Council, a forerunner of Skull and Bones ☠. A careful reading of history will
show you that the truly *chosen people* have been captured by
the beast and made eternally ignorant of their own purity.
African Americans are still not aware of their primordial existence. That reality has been removed from their soul through
a process called "intense education." They have been hit on
the head with "intense education" and buried in a subordinate
position, or grave. Amnesia causes them to serve an imposter,
instead of rising up to rule the world. The master thinks he is
the slave, and the slave thinks he is the master. The world has
been turned topsy-turvy.

## Rich Families

Who would have thought that rich families ran the world
and deliberately set up puppet Countries far from the original
throne, changing their names to hide so-called royal identity?
*Royal* is related to the word *regal* and *regal* is connected to the
word right, or righteous. Remember what the definition of
*Exxon* is? So how could a family be considered "royal" if it pro-
motes and devises diabolical schemes to subjugate the world?
Senator Tom Daschle has publicly complained about President Bush's Plan's to strengthen rich families at the expense
of poor people. There is a thin line between righteousness and
insanity. When I look at the news coming out of England or
Washington I do not see a righteous kingdom, I see *reptilian
style diplomacy.* American leaders from Yale University have
the same blood that makes the snake wind around the globe,
consuming everything in its path. By blood I could mean

mental aptitude. And you wonder why Asiatic people fear the upcoming war in Iraq or the open threats against Northern Korea, or Iran. Let me give you a short history lesson on the Tasker family and it will help you appreciate the shape of world power and how it is maintained, managed, and handled. You will see why this is important to the sniper case later. Let us go back three hundred years for the answer.

## Benjamin Tasker's Family

In this brief book the author will not have enough space to tell you all about the notorious history of Benjamin Tasker's family. Benjamin Tasker Middle School was where the shooting took place that would reveal the true intentions of the sniper. That shooting took place on October 7, 2002, the same day Benjamin Tasker's wife, Ann Bladen Tasker died in 1723. Governor Benjamin Tasker took office after his relative, Governor Samuel Ogle suddenly died in 1752. Benjamin Tasker was educated in England and he was a member of the Maryland Council. He lived on a plantation called "Belair." The British Empire had the entire East Coast under the control and influence of their family. Thus began the solidification of English rule in the New World. People had different names but they were of the same reptilian family.

This family owned slaves, raw material, and animals up and down the east coast. Governor Samuel Ogle was famous for introducing *thoroughbred horseracing* to North America "in English style." Cities and airports have been named after the Ogle Family. They don't call it the *Triple Crown* if you win all three races for nothing. *Triple* means three, and three equal lines make up the *triangle*, and *crown* represents royalty. Another member of their family owned the infamous slave ship named "Lord Ligonier." The bloodline in this family traces all the way back to so-called royal England, or English people, the group poising as *the chosen* and they are not (Rev 2:9). This same medieval family wants to totally dominate and manage the world through secret societies ☠. The biggest secret they hide is the true identify of the primordial people, Hebrews of African descent. African-Americans have no clue of their own royalty.

### John Ridout

John Ridout who was also a member of this affluent family owned the above-mentioned boat. Kunte Kinte was brought to America on this boat in 1767, and he was sold at Annapolis on October 7th. As you can see, October 7th keeps popping up. Afterwards the ship transported tobacco to London. In Maryland an elementary school is named after Samuel Ogle. This reality is an insult to African people. African American children are honoring the names of men who sold and killed their ancestors for profit, but nobody cares. The mentioning of this family, in passing, will make sense to you later in the reading of this entire document. But if you refuse to do your own investigative research you may not see the relevancy in pointing these peculiarities out in relation to the sniper case. I point these things out so that you can understand the symbolic nature of the shooting at Benjamin Tasker Middle School on October 7, 2002.

In the 1700's the dye was being set to rule the world for a thousand years. Again, the average person does not know about the spiritual contest being waged to dominate all aspects of planet earth, especially your lives. A very dangerous orchestra is playing a deadly song that destroys every one who hears it. War is the fuel that maintains this powerhouse, and many of you support it. Crime is the excuse to tighten the grip over the ignorant people, and many of you beg for tighter restrictions on your own lives. You do not understand how the

British Empire operates from behind the scenes on a global level (Ordo Ab Chao).

## The Invisible Hand

It is believed that the Bush Family is directly related to this so-called royal Family and many other previous presidents share the same bloodline. It is believed that George Washington was *raised* at the same Lodge as Benjamin Tasker, in Fredericksburg, Virginia. Some sources think that George Washington is not a blood relative, but that Lord Fairfax mentored him, and Lord Fairfax was a relative of Benjamin Tasker. Fairfax County is named after Lord Fairfax. George Washington was instrumental in forming "one Grand Lodge in America." "One" was spelled with a lower case "letter." This meant that the American Lodge was subordinate to The Grand Lodge of England. The revolutionary war threatened to shatter that umbilical cord. Somehow the baby had to be reconnected with its mother. General Lafayette made sure of that unique operation. *England must stay on top and the original thirteen states must obey its parent*. Both George Washington and General Lafayette's pictures adorn the upper chambers of the Lodge. Lord Baltimore, Proprietor of the Colony of Maryland is known to have given the Tasker family a painting by Philippe Mercier (1689-1760), called the four seasons. The four seasons have hidden within it the ineffable name of the Grand Architect of the Universe. Philippe Mercier was also the painter to the Prince of Wales. Hidden in the artwork are codes that must be deciphered by the elect. During the initial making of the United States many secret societies merged into one order. All of them together form one Lodge *(E Pluribus Unum)*. This was part of the *Master Plan*. You must read David Icke's book entitled "The Biggest Secret" for clarification. I warn you that this is the real "international mafia." George Washington is considered "the founding father of unified Masonry," not the founding father of the United States. In fact, the United States, as it is now, would not be realized until later. When George Washington was alive many states did not exist, so how could he be the founding father of California, Nevada, Arizona, etc. No, they are speaking over your head.

## George Bush, the Younger

George Bush, the younger, swore his oath of office on the same Masonic bible as George Washington, allegedly his distant relative. We know for sure that they are brothers in the Lodge if not in the flesh. There were several Benjamin Tasker's in the same family. The elder Tasker was educated in England but served as Governor of Maryland from 1798 till 1801. President Washington would consult with him on public matters, knowing he had a direct link to England. When you think of the "Psychology of Killing" all you see is "The Sniper," but many people see the conspiratorial parts to the 250-year-old puzzle being put together. I know you cannot see the connection right now, but hold on a few more chapters, and look around a few more days, you will see all that I am writing.

## The Honorable Elijah Muhammad

Another addition to the puzzle in the sniper case makes the killings seem to be ritual killings, instead of random acts of violence. The decoding of the anagram makes me want to look deeper into the possibility of a *global conspiracy*. You tell me how a member of the Nation of Islam could shoot a black child on the Honorable Elijah Muhammad's birthday? Wouldn't that strike you as odd? How can a member of the Nation of Islam shoot a child who is in transition to becoming a man (Bar Mitzvah)? The good-standing members of the rank and file that I know would never do such a thing. Some powerful group, well hidden, is really waging a psychological campaign against Islam and it is so obvious you cannot see it, for it is invisible. I am not a Muslim, but a blind man could see the abnormality of a Muslim desecrating the Messengers name by maliciously wounding a child on his birthday! No, these acts are more sinister, in my opinion. When I studied with the Nation of Islam they taught that, "The restricted laws of Islam will be your success." There is no success in violence, unless it is based on self-defense.

**My Question to You**

My question to you is why would someone pick Benjamin Tasker Middle School to up the ante in the sniper investigation? A school named after slaveholding families related to the British throne. The snipers path in the Washington area hit every County where the so-called Royal Family welded momentous power. Once Kenneth H. Bridges was killed the pattern of the killings formed a five-pointed star. The message left at the school had five stars drawn on a sheet of paper. This is something to think about. The *Tarot Card* that was left at the crime scene (XIII Death) is similar to the state seal of Virginia:

> A Knight in swarthy armor sits atop a pall horse, riding next to a dead king. The crown lies beyond the dead corpse as <u>the sun rises in the east</u> between two pillars. The Pope blesses the Skull and Bones ☠ that protect the horse's jugular veins with a gesture of "Branch to nose," a pagan ritual that few people understand. The flag the Knight holds in his left hand bares the number thirteen. Thirteen is very essential in Freemasonry and witchcraft. The flag is tied to a 'fascist pole.' The mother and child are at the mercy of the Skeleton- faced-Knight. I

*suggest that you compare this tarot card to Virginia's State seal and draw your own conclusion after looking for conspicuous similarities. Skull and Bones ☠, in their effort to dominate the world only allows organisms to live that maintain their power over the globe. The stark difference on the Virginia seal is a woman who kills the king. Few people know that the King is representative of African people. African people must never wear the global crown again. The Honorable Elijah Muhammad wore the crown sporting the Sun, Moon, and Stars. He was declaring his royalty without the permission of Europeans, and this made him dangerous to reptilian rule.*

The Knights Templars used the Skull ☠ in their ceremony of reception as a symbol of mortality and renewal. I would have to write another volume to show the significance of each County and State in relation to the homogeneity of the Tasker Family as it relates to clandestine (destination of clans) societies. What is even more interesting is the fact that these families prefixed their names with "The Honorable," a title of distinction. The Honorable Elijah Muhammad wanted the world to know that the Asiatic Black man was worthy of that distinction by nature. I stayed up for hours when this revelation entered my mind and troubled my soul. The little boy that got shot was around 13 years old. My antennas went up and I started paying close attention to Bowie, Maryland. The lady and child on the thirteenth Tarot Card can also represent the Virgin Mary and Child, or Mary Land (Maryland). The sniper wanted to sacrifice a child as he introduced mysticism into his crimes. The dead King who loses his crown would be representative of Virginia. This meant that from October 7th, 2002 the killer, or killers would remain within the circumference of Virginia and Maryland until caught. The guy that was shot at the Ponderosa Steak House in Ashland, Virginia took place on England Street. The rays from the sun meant the sniper was following the pagan god of the dead (eulogia), not the Honorable Elijah Muhammad. Let us now complete the Benjamin Tasker family tree.

## John Taylor

John Taylor, another one of Benjamin Tasker's family owned Iron Works up and down the East Coast where enslaved people were made to work from sun up until sun down. His estate lay next to the James River, Greenway. He would always put articles in the newspapers when his slaves ran away, and a massive manhunt would follow. A few of his enslaved were hung after the American Revolution; they were accused of taking up arms against the Commonwealth. America is a country with a very violent history and we wonder why people resort to using violence in modern times. I believe this same John Taylor's son would become president. Violence today is a curse from the past. I feel that the truth must be told about how America became a bitter nation saturated with frustration, violence, and death. This same John Taylor may be one of the signers of the Constitution (May to September 1787 in Philadelphia).

## Billy Taylor

Billy Taylor, John Taylor's enslaved black man, ran away several times before the revolution. He would _forge fake passes_ and invite himself to celebrations, _cross state lines,_ and play his violin at white parties to earn fees that he said his master requested for his service. During these adventures he would unlawfully barrow his so-called master's horse. Evidence suggests that Billy was half white, a mulatto, and this gave him certain artificial privileges. Many believe that Billy was also related to the 'Taylor family' by blood. Someone misinformed Billy that if he made it to South Caroline he would be free. At some point Billy decided to fight for his liberation and he took up arms against his own Country. George Washington was totally against blacks being in the United States Army and drafted legislation-forbidding blacks to re-enlist. The British, on the other hand, welcomed blacks into their ranks and they promised liberty to any blacks that fought on their side. Billy was John Taylor's most famous enslaved who was hung at the Common Gallows for fighting on the side of the British in 1781. How can you sign a Constitution guaranteeing your freedom, but kill a man for fighting for his freedom? There is a record somewhere in Richmond, Virginia showing how many people were hung at the Common Gallows during that time, but historians are reluctant to uncover that information. Their constituents would not be pleased at such an exposé.

## The Common Gallows

The Common Gallows was located at 15th and Broad Street in Richmond, Virginia. And 19 years later Gabriel Prosser was hung there too, you guessed it, in October, 1800. Today, that sight is a parking lot for the Medical College of Virginia. Virginia Commonwealth University is secretly exhuming some of those bodies buried at that sight to determine the ethnicity of the victims among other things. Dr. Philip Schwarz is heading or involved in an investigation surrounding the history of "The Gallows." I suspect they want to find Gabriel Prosser to do some DNA test on him since some of his family still resides in the area. I recently discovered that Comrade Prosser served time for stealing a pig from somebody, and thought of overthrowing the slave system while in jail. But Billy's head was cut off and hung from a pole at a public crossroad before he could realized that freedom was do him, so everyone could see it in 1781 dangling from above. Prince William County was where the trial took place. This is the same county where the sniper will be judged for declaring war on the American people. It would take further research for me to determine if this so-called slave-master is the same John Taylor who wrote *"An Inquiry into the principles and policy of the Government"* in 1814. If so, he was a member of the Virginia House of Delegates and a United States Senator. This is why I marvel when I hear ignorant people fussing and complaining about Senator Trent Lott's opinions on segregation, but they never say anything about their children going to schools named after people who owned, degraded, and hung blacks from poles with their heads decapitated! As a matter of fact, our children are made to be loyal to these schools named after killers and slave owners. What type of game is being played on African Americans? In modern times we are still being *hoodwinked*. Senator Trent Lott is forced to step down and Senator Bill Frist is made Republican leader of the house. The amazing thing is the similarity in their voting history. You would think a person with a meager education would figure this game out by now. Senator Bill Frist votes almost identical to Senator Trent Lott.

## Formal Education

It is obvious that *formal education* has been denied the black race in many respects. Would a quasi-Jew go to a school named after Himmler? I don't think so! Many so-called leaders have *selective sensitivity* and will only grumble about certain issues, but steer clear of controversial topics. In a quick research effort I discovered that Benjamin Tasker and his clan are directly related to the British Crown. This was how and why they all went to England for a formal education on how to conserve the Crown through inheritance and deception.

The same family continues to rule through secret societies and Ivy League commissions put together to preserve the union. Malcolm X called it the "International combine." The *Trilateral Commission* is an offshoot of those early societies.

## Western Europe

The *Trilateral Commission* boast of being a non-Governmental, policy-oriented discussion group of about 350 prominent citizens from Western Europe, North America and Pacific Asia, allegedly formed to advance mutual understanding between all concerned and to recommend foreign policy. At the grassroots level we suspect that they weld too much power over our lives and many of us only have superficial information on what they actually do. If you are not connected to some financial empire, or related to the so-called royal family of Europe, then certain information is kept from you and your brain is taught to function on an elementary level (sub-human level). You never learn the physics of life, or organism (Organizations). Skull and Bones ☠ is an offshoot of this same family but you lack enough information to figure it out, and they exist primarily undetected. They teach their members the significance of symbols as it relates to world dominance. When a man joins Skull and Bones ☠ he takes a picture in front of a grandfather clock, a human skull and Bones ☠ sits atop a *roundtable*, the time machine in the back is set at *8 o-clock am*, fourteen other candidates' poise with him. A total of 15 men are present during this ritualistic initiation. The spider and the octopus have eight legs used to kill its enemies, and this is why the clock is set at eight.

The car the snipers purchased from *Sure Shot Auto shop* for $250 dollars had 15,000,000 miles on it and Kenneth Harold Bridges was the eight shooting victim in the Washington area killing spree. Was his life squeezed away by the eight-legged octopus? Did the car have 15, 000,000 to represent the 15 candidates in the order? Or are these numbers simply coincidental? I cannot answer that for you. I am merely trying to get you to think outside the box.

## The Brotherhood of Death

If the general population was not concerned about these numbers, Skull and Bones ☠ understood the esoteric nature of what was occurring. The shape of the killings meant something to them, even if they did not inform the general public. *'The Brotherhood of death'* knows everything about the dying, and what they don't tell you are simply what they do not want you to know. What is more important is the fact that they know you will not believe me. It's not about informing you anyway; it is about controlling you. They hold key positions in every agency that involves human control. As long as you remain ignorant, they win. In Freemasonry the triangle symbolized the Tetragrammaton or the ineffable name of the Creator. Many biblical scholars pronounce the four letters as 'Yahweh.' If you can visit the Grand Lodge in Europe you will visibly see the Hebraic "yod" sign written backwards in their main chamber. This signifies that the truth will be revealed backwards to the ignorant masses, but straight forward to the elect, as those who know move forward, and those who do not know, fall backwards.

## Sacrificial Lamb

Behaviorally, you can say the triangle has something to do with 'righteousness and evil.' Obviously, the killer understood pictograms and symbols too. If you have a piece of plastic turn it over and look at the triangular shaped recycle symbol in the form of arrows. The *Trilateral Commission* uses a similar symbol for its organization. The object or container has been brought back from the dead. At one time it was useless and now it is usable. What does the triangle mean to the decoder of ancient symbols? *It means somebody innocent has to die so that someone who is guilty can live.* Whenever one is crucified another is weighed and found wanting. Think of Yahshua and the two thieves on the stake. This is the scale of life that few people understand. Perhaps the shape of the killing spree that spread across America in the sniper case was coincidental and did not mean anything at all. Otherwise, we can surmise that the triangular killings could have been another clue of something deeper, bigger, and more sinister. The kind of message designed only for a select few to comprehend. This book will challenge what you are not thinking and will question what you have been taught to think by mainstream education. Hopefully, you will look at world events somewhat differently. When dots are drawn on maps for the entire world to see you will understand that each dot tells a story and unlocks a mystery. Most of our people are afraid to crack mysteries because they have been made to think spooky. Years of physical abuse and threats have stymied our inquisitive nature. The institution of slavery caused fear to be stored genetically in our veins, and we dare not question those in Authority. This book only unlocks one dot. I do not have the time or resources to unlock each dot. It only took three weeks to unlock the hidden code of one dot. That is the dot of Benjamin Tasker Middle School.

## Global Occupation

You could draw a line from Washington State to Alabama, up to Montgomery County, Maryland and then connect it back to Tacoma, Washington where the killings started earlier this year. Do not underestimate patterns, symbols, and anagrams.

In a strange way it looks like the sale of rum, molasses, and human cargo back when Sir John Hawkins worked in cahoots with Queen Elizabeth, using her ship named "Jesus" to profit off of the largest continental kidnappings the earth ever saw. One was a quasi-Jew and the other an English woman; they both benefited from the suffering and wholesale relocation of *Cushite People*. This illegal trade deal was the beginning of *Global Occupation*. I am not sure if the killer set out to draw this picture of a triangle with dead corpses or a five-pointed star. But since it was drawn that way someone must comment on it. A few years ago a white male orchestrated a series of mail bombing that drew a picture of a gigantic smile. I guess you could label him a geographic artistic killer (GAK) wanting to make a point within a circle of confusion (Ordo Ab Chao).

Let us go back to the triangular slave trade route. Since that time only Caucasian entrepreneurs were granted *International Trade Agreements* that allowed them to maintain their economic superiority over others. If you did trade with Africa, the Caucasoid man got his money first, and you might get some crumbs from his *roundtable* later. The Anglo-Saxon monopoly would not allow Africans like Marcus Garvey to become independent of them without a fatal brawl or expatriation. The Honorable Marcus Garvey was forced out of the country with the help of the NAACP when he strove for the economic liberation of black folk. You would be shocked to discover how the Boule helped to remove Marcus Garvey from America. I suggest you study the teachings of Steve Cokely for that information. Brother Steve has done a wonderful job exposing the Boule.

## Caucasian Monopoly

We still underestimate the racist practice of Caucasian monopoly over our lives. In fact, we think we are totally free even though we struggle economically as a nation within a nation. Every negative situation that America has the black man suffers disproportionately greater than anyone else. This reality engenders a deep psychological anxiety in the minds of unconscious African-Americans, and extreme cases produce a "Psychology of Killing." We are aware that many commerce laws as written in the *Uniform Commercial codes* are designed to give Anglo-Saxon people the advantage over their competitors. I suppose you do not know who his competitor is? It is you and I. You should ask yourself what a chauvinistic institution would do to maintain power over you. The answer is "whatever it takes." Would it create a vicious cycle of violence to keep you forever subordinate to your former slave master? Yes it would! Niccolo Machiavelli wrote extensively on how statesmen utilize power and what they must do to maintain power. There is a formula that keeps you and I entangled economically. A few Caucasian people are privileged to have an institution that guarantees their dominance over all people and they are not about to give that privilege up without a fight. The new Nano-technology will guarantee their rule one thousand more years. Bill Clinton spent one billion dollars on Nano-systems development and President Bush put up another $700 million through his administration. They have used this technology to create clothing that makes them invisible, and bullet proof. *Once you become invisible it increases your chances of becoming invincible.* In the future the world will be fighting ghost, literally. Bullets will be programmed to chase down targets, even if the victim turns multiple corners, or hide behind concrete slabs. Weapons specialists are working on hand held guns that shoot 12-inch metal pipes two miles per second with precise accuracy. How would you catch a sniper who shoots from 2-miles away? You do not understand how killings benefit the so-called elite class! Each man that dies prematurely from violence guarantees the so-called elite class rule over you another day.

## Inverted Turmoil

Whenever governments fight against the progress of its own people, by mass-producing vehicles of death, citizens fight against themselves. I term this kind of conflict "inverted turmoil." It is easier to take your frustration out on unarmed civilians than for you to challenge the greatest *"Military Industrial Complex"* on earth. You have a better chance stealing from your poor brother, then to take from the *Internal Revenue Service*, the organization that takes billions from you each year without explanation. Your lack of consciousness allowed you to participate in building a *pathological machine* that will strangle us slowly to death with transparent reptilian hands. Your own people will try to slaughter you to ensure the continuation of this breed of Saturnalian militarized dictatorship coming out of WASHINGTON D.C. Subsequently, the people are becoming just as cold and heartless as this innovative machine that traffics in death. I am referring to a machine that runs off the juices of secret societies.

## Benjamin Banneker City

It would take time for the elongated murder spree to make sense, as if senseless killings could ever make sense. As the killings increased and ping-pong balled up and down Interstate 95, fear became noticeable on the faces of patriotic and not so patriotic Americans alike. It seemed as though the cases that were piling up would never be solved as bodies dropped at gas stations, stores, parking lots, and one Haitian man while simply walking down the street in *Benjamin Banneker's City*. Prostrate corpses stretched across the evening news as anxiety escalated. At one time the killer would even strike in close proximity to a Virginia State Police. All of this is "inverted turmoil" produced out of centuries of racism and neglect.

### The Brazen Serpent

The sniper was becoming "brazen" like a "serpent" and extremely cold. Criminal psychologist was puzzled and had a difficult time trying to comprehend the psychological make up of the killer or killers who meandered near Quantico, Virginia. Once the FBI lady (Linda Franks) was fatally wounded while standing next to her husband, no one felt out of harm's way again. Why was she killed? What was the real motivation behind the killings? Were any of the targets deliberate? It is very important that a "think tank" committee who are not biased, and cannot be controlled by big dollars, or other loyalties answer this question. The entire sniper case rings of conspiracy.

### The 911 Commissions

The *Trilateral Commission* cannot answer this question for the grassroots people. The *911 Commission* will not answer this question and the *NAACP* is not interested in delving into the inner workings of secret societies. We want poor people to answer this question who you consider uneducated. People like me who have never been brainwashed in institutions of higher confusion. The same ones you accuse of being over-sensitive and paranoid. You must accept the fact that so-called professionals only profess to have theories, not facts. Common sense is not an optional course in college. You simply go to these institutions to get further in debt. The process of education in the English schools is geared towards making you loyal to the king in robotic fashion, solidifying your slave state of mind.

I know this book is beginning to sound hostile. You would sound hostile too, symbolically speaking, if your government was instigating wars and conflicts all over the globe! I thank Yahweh that my hostility is communicated through literature, not delivered through bullets. Our world must really look at the violent course it has embarked on! Let us return to the sniper-case analysis.

## Professional Speculators

Professional speculators or profilers would race to the National and International cameras and place their bet on the profile of the killer. Retired specialist scurried down to the local T.V station to put in their conjectures.  Almost unanimously they guessed that the killer was an intelligent 'white man' with some military experience. He must be calculating and precise. Knowing how to handle a rifle with steady hands and hitting his target in vital areas that rush the clock towards death. You may want to ask yourself why they see *white men* as killers.

## Western World

Deep down inside, and consciously too, we all know what the white man is capable of doing when he feels threatened. The psychopathic personality trait is more prevalent and common in the suburbs among middle-class white men who get laid off from a lucrative career, then a destitute black man who is called a failure. Think about the white man in Georgia who hammered his family to death, and then went to his office and killed his fellow co-workers after his stocks dropped significantly. Jeffrey Dahmer and Gary Schaefer are perfect examples of my point, but I am very aware that black men are deteriorating psychologically in the Western world. This deterioration is causing them to purchase guns and shoot people.

We are developing the same mentality as white folk, killing, robbing, exploiting, and taking advantage of people with no shame. We really need to examine what America has turned us into.

## The Usual Profile

In the last two decades we have read about black men killing passengers on commuter trains, shooting people at their place of employment, and randomly inflicting violence on elderly people and others. You would think that with all the murders in the inner city, with the black on black homicide, police would first think of young black man when multiple killings are involved these days. Despite the rise among black criminals in America, white men are still seen as the most dangerous killers, the most vicious when it come to numerous killings for no apparent reason. Law enforcement usually profile white men in serial murder cases; I might add, could this be because black men do not generally go after innocent people? In drive-by shootings, from time to time, innocent people do get hit for being in the wrong place at the wrong time. I have read of little children being killed in the hood while being in the line of fire, but this is not a common practice among black people. Most killings in high-stressed and poverty-stricken neighborhoods are the result of personal squabbles, bad drug deals, anger, and the violence is usually directed at a specific target. I hope the Washington-area sniper case is not showing the world how we, the former enslaved, have fully assimilated, or integrated, and now depreciated to the level of our former master! The old cowboy movies are coming to life.

However, the professional investigators understand that violence is new, or fairly new, to black communities. There was a time here in America when the only violent act inflicted on black communities came from white men who controlled our neighborhoods. My question to you is whom are black men imitating now since our communities have been abandoned by big business? Dis-investment is ruining our neighborhoods and killing our self-esteem. People have more respect for well-kept places, than they do for dilapidated places. During my destitute investigation, I was visiting the University of Virginia and discovered the same "Skull and Bone" ☠ symbol on one of the fraternity houses on campus.

### Went Berserk

I wonder if John Allen Muhammad found evidence of the New World Order and went berserk, completely lost his mind? What was his reason for emphasizing "Skull and Bones" ☠ on the stolen laptop? Why was he keeping a diary that would implicate or incriminate him? Will the public ever have access to his final entries? Did he mention others in his entries that would show a global mission? Was he brainwashed to carry out this military assignment and promised money? Did he have an implant inserted in his brain when he was in the military? The way the system is designed you will never get the answers to these essential inquires. The juvenile suspect told a young lady down south that they were "working for the secret intelligence." Is that what John Allen Muhammad told him to say or was he telling the truth? Will this critical piece of evidence be investigated just as thoroughly as the 223-calibre bullet? I don't think so. It will be pushed to the side like a piece of burnt toast. I think it will be difficult finding out about the snipers connections to the New World Order.

### What about Bush?

If in fact President George Bush is a member of a clandestine group, what role does it play in the control of the world? What would be the meaning of the "Skull" Symbol? ☠ Anatomically we know that the "skull" protects the mind and the mind protects the body. The "bone" supports the body and allows it to move about the earth. However, the "skull" cannot operate without flesh, blood, and food. And the "bones" cannot move without the benefit of the brain. If you pull back the layers of skin you discover the life of a living organism. Depending on the health of the body, you can determine the longevity of its life span, and you can know where the vital organs are located. Most importantly, you can know the nature of the organism through closer examination.

## Psychopathic Personality

Initially, law enforcement was not willing to look towards black men in a case of such vicious magnitude. Only white men could or should be capable of shutting down interstates, invade the imagination of the populace, outsmart the police, master assault riffles, aim once and hit the target, perfect the art of killing, cause wide-spread panic and fear, and erase innocent people from the living. Death is too much power in the hands of Negroes.

Only the likes of the charismatic Ted Bundy, Henry Lee Lucas, the artistic John Wayne Gacy or the talkative Timothy McVeigh could be ingenious enough to pull such a crime off. What is it about the white man that targets him as a possible serial killer, or a primary suspect whenever it comes to a deadly killing spree? Do white people know something about themselves that we do not know? If, or when, people are randomly dying from violence it must be a white man doing the killing, according to forensic specialist. Or at least this is what the professional profilers would have us believe. I attribute this to the violent history of white men, from lynches that scared black communities into not competing with their white counterparts during reconstruction, to America's bloody past with the natives, and her dropping the Atomic Bomb on Japan twice.

The sniper is a person who suffers from the "psychopathic personality" and has tendencies to hurt and kill people, according to the loquacious specialist on one local station. In addition, "he has no sympathy for human suffering." One expert said the "white man was married and suffered from sexual abnormalities." Based on undisclosed evidence left at the crime scenes they determined fairly quickly that the crimes were not connected to a terrorist outfit like Hamas or the Lebanese party of Hezbollah. The author believes that this determination was made only after the October 7, shooting at Benjamin Tasker Middle School. This is the reason why I concentrated on this particular school. This school will be discussed further when the anagram is exposed. I have already given you some clues about the importance of this date, the name of school, and its connection to rich families in America. The number seven in the numerology chart means mysticism, psychic, and magic. *You fight not against flesh and blood, but against principalities and powers in high places.* In the original teachings as taught by the Nation of Islam seven means "God." As a person who is familiar with the teachings, I must admit that my antennas went up when the suspect announced, "Dear Mister Policemen, I am god," on the Seventh Day of October. This is not just any old day for members in the Nation of Islam. To attempt to pervert the teachings through violence inflicted on a young 13-year-old black boy on the Messengers birthday is beyond insane. It is sacrilegious to commit a violent act on the messenger's birth date. Noble Drew Ali, The Honorable Elijah Muhammad, Marcus Garvey, Brother Malcolm X, and Minister Louis Farrakhan would never have approved of such foolishness coming from its ranks. Someone is really trying to bring *"shame and disgrace"* to the Nation of Islam in these last days. Whoever financed the snipers movements in and out of the Country must be working for a giant network beyond the reach of local law enforcement.

## Zionist Occupation Government (ZOG)

Islamic Freedom Fighters publicize their attacks and state reasons that justify their fighting determination in their minds. So-called professionals think, "There is an archaic culture of violence that drives the Islamic world." Therefore, when a militant Muslim kills a target it is accepted and announced publicly in certain Islamic countries. Just like "The Army of Palestine" quickly claimed responsibility for the Mombasa, Kenya attacks that killed 16 people on Thanksgiving Day, 2002. They don't hesitate to publicize their organizational sponsorship when they kill people because they feel justified in fighting for their faith. Immediately after the Paradise Hotel terror campaign the *"Government of Universal Palestine"* said *"the strikes were designed to mark the anniversary of the Nov. 29, 1947 U.N. decision to partition Palestine into Jewish and Arab states."* You would have to understand how Muslims feel about Zionist Occupation Governing (ZOG) their homeland to feel the passion of their cause. Palestinian occupation is what the Wahhabist base their interpretation of Islamic verse on.

You can read the article by Neil MacFARQUHAR, dated December 24, 2002 in The New York Times, on Hezbollah. Muslims in Lebanon call the Bush Doctrine "Satanic." So why did the sniper use Judaic symbols to communicate with a Christian Nation about Islamic frustrations in a secular world? The tarot card is Jewish, America is a Christian nation, and John Muhammad is a Muslim. This is the main reason I find it difficult to see their logic in confessing to a Catholic priest in Ashland, Virginia. None of it makes sense.

## Philosophy of Israel

I wonder if the sniper understood that the occult philosophy of Israel is connected to the Tarot Cards. Is it possible that he was fighting against their rule in the Middle East in his mind? This is not to imply that the sniper was justified in his actions. I feel that he was totally unjustified! I simply am trying to illustrate what his mind may have been thinking if he is the sniper. You would be surprised how many people disagree with Israel's military regime, but they do not go out killing innocent people. I recommend you read a book by former Senator Paul Findley entitled "They Dare to Speak Out" for a better appreciation of the protagonist who helped to shape and maintain a criminal enterprise that attempts to use religiosity to subjugate natives. This illegal enterprise is what influences the beast-like nature in mankind to express itself with bombs and ammunition.

## Quasi-Jews

It is not Justice to take someone's land two thousand years later, without concrete proof that it was your ancestors land in the first place. No well-read person of world affairs, or history, believes the quasi-Jews have right to Palestine. The quasi-Jews did not name their hotel situated in Kenya "*paradise*" for nothing. They know that the African people are the original Hebrews, the primordial race. And they know that the British are not the chosen people. What would it benefit the *occupational forces* to tell their former captives who the real master is? In many aspects so-called liberal media never gives the truth to us. Your brain has not been conditioned to quiz "why would the quasi-Jews name a hotel "paradise" that was situated in Africa? Could it be that they just might know who you are in relation to Yahweh? When will quasi-Jews and

Caucasians admit that people of African descent are the original people and that the true *House of Yahweh* was located in Africa, not Jerusalem? This truth will erase the *mentality* that causes our youth to kill one another for no apparent reason. If the younger sniper suspect knew his true identity he would be helping to heal people, not working to kill people.

## Blasphemy

The public was never told the reason why a sniper would kill people, apparently at random. The first clue that leaked to the public was a written statement from the killer or killers saying, "Dear Mr. Policeman, I am god." An orthodox Muslim would never call himself "god." That would be blasphemous in the Islamic World. "There is no god, but Allah," is a famous utterance from the faithful, but never a pronouncement of being "god." A member of al-Qaida would say, "Allah is the Greatest." They would never say, "I am god." They may not commit blasphemy because it is against their faith to make anyone equal with *The Almighty*. In some Islamic countries to call oneself "god" is a capital offense and you may be beheaded in the public square for saying such a thing. And yet, they are permitted to blast some innocent child away in their fight against oppression, according to some extreme groups. I am referring to the fanatic who calls himself a Muslim, Jew, or Christian, and who is willing to die or kill for his belief. I am referring to the type that think all humans should think and worship as they do. No innocent blood is justified in a fight for freedom if it can be prevented. I respect all religions, so if a religious zealot does something to me mark him off as a demon.

When a religious fanatic thinks that any act is justified in carrying out his faith, he becomes a fool, the kind of person who is incapable of thinking for the benefit of his own longevity or his people. In a selfish way they blow themselves up, shoot innocent people, which is also murder in the sight of *The Almighty*. He becomes a combatant for an unrighteous cause. What type of philosophy can convince a person to blow himself up and kill innocent people in a war that has no winners and no end?

## Collateral Damage

The military of all countries believe that civilian causalities are inevitable in warfare and necessary for psychological impact. All countries have a group of young men whom they train to kill and be killed. They are "Toy soldiers who destroy for the puppet master." In the Persian Gulf John Allen Muhammad was one of these "toy soldiers."

If civilians die when America bombs a building in Iraq, during the upcoming Persian Gulf War, then the target will be thought to be an Iraqi Command Post, thus making the victims casualties of war, and the death becomes justified in the military community. But will the death be truly justified? Absolutely not!

Two quasi-Jewish children died in the Kenyan explosion mentioned above. Emphasis is never placed on how many Africans die from terrorism. All children are innocent and only a coward will make them his targets. It would be nice if Israel would take a closer look at their attitudes towards the Muslim Natives and how this engenders hatred. There is no question about Palestinians being their neighbors, even if the Neo-Jews (post-1948) did take the land by force after allegedly being gone for two thousand years. Imagine the American Natives wanting their land back from the white man after three hundred years of forced exile. Would Israel support that geographically centered argument coming from the so-called American Indians?

## Global Protection

No race should have to die over ancient traditions. Religion can always be used to justify brutality and racial violence can be ignored if the victims are less valuable to the corporate cause. There is a thin line between righteousness and insanity. The line is even thinner when Africans are victimized disproportionately. Look how the world is reacting because Caucasians are being murdered in this century. Africans have suffered genocide over the last 450 years and their remains no reaction, no justice, and no protective policies. The international power structure can kill all Africans in 21 days because only the *"International Combine"* can produce weapons of mass destruction for its global protection. And you want to understand the "Psychology of Killing?" Or do you really want to maintain your dominance over the world another thousand years? Is that what this re-mapping, revamping and global-military-positioning is all about?

## Foreign Policy

America must not shed innocent blood when she fights her self-made enemies, or her self-made enemies will harm American civilians in retaliation. Secret societies ⚥ formulated policy to enrage Islamic countries over a 14-hundred year period, from the Knights of Malta to the Knights of Columbia, and some Muslims are tired of being victims of so-called Caucasian supremacy that affects every facet of their lives. African Americans have brought in to their victimization and will only sing about a world of equality (We shall overcome). We have been conditioned to think that Caucasians have a legitimate right to rule our lives, so we subconsciously look down at anyone struggling to be free. Some Muslims have taken up arms to reclaim their dignity and power. But that fight looks very ugly to the enslaved.

If you preach "Justice" let your actions be Just! How can you teach *'peace'* and practice *'destruction?'* Isn't that a contradiction? Racist Foreign policy can be just as violent as Kamikaze airplanes flying into skyscrapers in the center of New York City. We don't want terrorist killing civilians over here, and they do not want Uncle Sam killing their people over there! Uncle Sam kills through embargoes, sanctions, usurpation, exploitation, unfair trading practices, and outright threats.

*Before these terrorist acts, millions of Americans were converting to Islam, seeking a more humane way to live. The American power structure really felt vulnerable after the Million Man March. It was a peaceful demonstration of mass discontent. Change is more permanent in peace time- there is no compulsion in Islam to proselytize the world, according to the doctrine. It appears that someone had to stop this rise in Islam on American shores, by any means necessary. Accomplish this even if it means starting a war against the Islamic world, or programming a Muslim to kill innocent people with an implant that controls behavior.*

Stop trying to change the world through violence, force, and threat! Today's Muslims must not revert to the Crusader-tactics that President Bush loves to boast about, privately and publicly. Our entire world has lost something dear: it is called humanity. This may be the wild-wild-west and the President may hunt down his enemies, but we have come too far to lose everything over a family squabble. The rich families in Arabia and the rich families in Europe must not put their toy soldiers on the battlefield; the consequences are too great these days!

## Antagonistic Faith

As a conscious person I see all religions as potentially antagonistic and contradictory. Muslims and Christians that condone violence, or refuse to condemn unwarranted violence, are not setting a righteous example and I do not think you are following a righteous man. If Prophet Mohammed (PBUH) or Prophet Yahshua (PBUH) condoned this type of evil I would not want to follow them. I cannot believe they were that way. No, you are following the lust of your own heart. I refuse to believe that Prophet Mohammed (PBUH) or Prophet Yahshua (PBUH) would order the death of innocent people, especially with the beastlike brutality that terrorist and crusaders have implemented in the name of both prophets over the last two thousand years. Politics do not fair any different in my book. Killing in the name of George Washington, the so-called *founding father of unified Masonry* is just as fanatic! What did our government do to cause half the world to hate us so much? What fools in their right mind thinks that democracy is the best system produced by mankind? There is a better system waiting for the younger generation to produce it. It is called "*human appreciation and respect for all systems, for all beliefs, and peoples.*"

I dare you to start looking for the answer to the above question and after statement. It will help you understand the "psychology of killing." When innocent people die in suicide bombings, the bomber goes straight to hell, figuratively speaking. Once innocence is violated it is no longer a "holy war." It becomes an act of Satan, figuratively speaking. This goes for suicide bombers that murder civilians at bus stops in Israel and American pilots who drop bombs on civilian targets in Iraq, or Afghanistan. How many civilians do you think America killed in Hiroshima and Nagasaki? If there is a concept called "Justice" who will have to pay for the crimes of the past? Civilians were slaughtered in Vietnam too. Over one hundred million African civilians died coming to this country in the middle passage. We must really look deep within ourselves if we want to rid the world of the mindset that engenders vicious conduct! There is room for all of us to forgive and move forward. Every country needs to repent and ask The Almighty for forgiveness, especially America.

## Violent Potentiality

All people have the potential to be truculent, even Americans. No one has given America and Britain the right to police the world and the world does have the right to reject her bulldozing activities and dictatorial mentality. What ever occurred to the original purpose of the United Nations? It was supposed to be a place where all nations decide on decisions of geopolitical substance. After Nazi-Germany no nation was to function unilaterally to subdue another nation militarily. Go back and read the papers from the Geneva Convention and the United Nations Charter that Malcolm X talked about before his assassination.

## Distorted Mind

Was the sniper fighting against this New World Order in his own distorted mind? The sniper would prove repeatedly how violent Americans could get in Northern Virginia. I hope the sniper case is not indicative of the voiceless inhabitants of the world needing to be desperately heard and going to extremities to get their point across. "Desperate times produce desperate people." I also hope the sniper was not given this assignment by secret societies � who promised him protection and money. The average person would not even fathom this possibility. As a matter of fact, the average person does not know that snipers are trained to produce "One Shot, One Kill." The cadence song they sang when running in place at Fort Benning, Georgia says "one shot, one kill" repeatedly. They wear the same kind of shirt the younger suspect allegedly had on in a picture that was released to the press. The black shirt has a target right on the heart, and it reads "sniper."

## One Shot, One Kill

Behind closed doors sheriffs, forensic pathologists, homicide detectives, FBI agents and ATF workers had already surmised that the killings were that of a disgruntled 'white man' in his early or mid-twenties. While these officers were working overtime trying to guess the nature of the crimes the sniper or snipers were loading up and aiming to kill repeatedly with one shot.

The Washington area sniper occurrence would mesmerize the East Coast and almost paralyze two states as well as the District of Columbia. Politicians and their advisors quickly jumped inside the Trojan Horse of media discourse and entered the fray of public opinion. Law enforcement officers worked night and day trying to catch the killer or killers, to no avail. The expedition would translate into the biggest Manhunt in United States history. The last time a man was hunted so thoroughly in that region of America was when Negroes ran from slave plantations like the one owned by John Taylor. Even the escape from Mecklenburg Correctional Center's death row in 1984 was miniscule when compared to the sniper escapade and the dragnet that followed. Before this investigation is over it will have cost taxpayers millions of dollars.

## MKULTRA: Cia Mind Control

During the initial stages of the investigation there were many questions. Was the killer white, Asian, or Black? Did the killer suffer from some perverted Oedipus complex or neurotic disorder that caused him to strike out maliciously? Was there a political connection to the assaults? Was he a single man or did he have a family? Was he a vagabond or did he live in the area? Was the killer a victim of "MKULTRA: CIA Mind Control or was he acting on his own volition?" No one would believe a person could be brainwashed to act other than himself. And yet, people are suing restaurant chains for making them obese, and tobacco companies for making them smoke. When a black man kills he is totally responsible for his actions. Only white killers are afforded the brainwashing defense. Patty Hurst was given leniency for not being of herself when robbing banks during the Cultural Revolution in the 70's, or brainwashed, according to some reports. The insanity defense will not be considered in the sniper case.

I repeat, did someone give the mercenary the order to kill certain people and promised him a substantial amount of money in the end? Why did the killer demand $10 million near the end of his killing spree? Was that the amount he was promised to do the job? Out of all the people killed, which victim played a significant role on an International level? Were the murders intended to interfere with the economic liberation of black people? If you are a true revolutionary thinker you must form "think tanks" to answer these questions as soon as you put this book down. Stop allowing White media and Black Boule-minded-Negroes to shape your opinions! Even your most radical leaders should not be exempt from scrutiny when a black leader dies a violent death.

## Kenneth H. Bridges

I am very troubled that a powerful man like Kenneth Harold Bridges was struck down and no black leader is questioning the conspiratorial nature of his assassination! Brother Ken was working on our economic freedom when he died on route one, from one shot. I wonder if the other victim's had been a decoy simply to eliminate Brother Ken. Or did the killer simply go ballistic and kill everything in his sight? The author is also wondering why the killers allegedly struck a Jewish synagogue in Washington State, Temple Bethel. In front of Temple Bethel there is a sign with the Star of David shown conspicuously on it. Was this the inverted and upright pyramid that announced the beginning of chaos? I hope this is not a case of a secret agent ☠ carrying out an assignment to usher in a New World Order and then being dropped like a hot potato off route 70.

## Critical Questions

We need to question everybody's intent. What is it about our thinking that allows us to underestimate the nature of the enemy ☠ when it comes to the destruction of black men or the maintenance of power? If we fail to follow this case thoroughly and seek answers to these critical questions, we may miss the neo-methods used by the enemy to assassinate our key leaders or destroy our creditability. There has never been a genuine investigation into the death of Dr. Khalid Abdul Muhammad, Dr. Martin Luther King, Malcolm X, Dr. Huey P. Newton, and now Dr. Kenneth Bridges. I am surprised that so-called black leaders are not speaking out about these possibilities. Was the sniper operating alone or was he carrying out orders from some international guerrilla outfit? There seems to be no answers to the myriad of questions. As a scholar of questionable activity on the part of our so-called democratic government, a government that has skillfully disenfranchised the black vote, I will continue to ask questions even if you falsely label me Anti-American. And I do not care how many black people dislike me for being a thinker! More white people will agree with what I am speculating than black people. Modern Negroes still have the fear of the whip on their mind.

## The Great Satan

Was the killer or killers connected to Al-Qaidi or some other radical group that prays for the destruction of America and Israel, The so-called Great Satan? By the end of the week, back in October 2002, the killings seemed to be at random and the motivation remained unclear. Was the sniper the type of Muslim that believes that "Jihad is his mission," and the killing is the prerequisite to freedom for the Islamic world? But nobody could figure out the mind of the person, or persons, behind the gun with 223 projectile capabilities. Some thought he was a dormant, or *sleeper* type mechanic carrying out his assignment. I say he got caught ten times and was let go each time. Either he was part of something bigger, or we got a very ignorant intelligence agency working to protect us.

## District of Columbia

A year earlier the District of Columbia was trying to put a stop to the deadly anthrax scare that threatened to shut down the mailing system and had barely recovered from that terror, or may not have improved from it at all, and now a sniper was causing worse fears to surface in the minds of the people. America had already suffered a horrendous blow as a result of the terrorist attacks relating to September 11, 2001. We, as a nation, had already forgotten about what took place in Africa a few years earlier. It truly amazes me that African-Americans felt no pain or sympathy when the two Embassies in Kenya were blown to smithereens on August 7, 1998! In fact, no one remembers that date these days. Forty-six years earlier Malcolm X was released from prison on August 7, 1952. *He went to prison a "confused Christian and left prison a very intelligent Muslim," according to one of his televised interviews in the early 60's.* Malcolm X's contribution to Islam is unmatched in North America, with the exception of his teacher. Again, the lives of blacks have no value in some black people's mind. Why would they remember the day Malcolm X was paroled or the day Kenya was bombed? These historical occurrences have no meaning to modern Negroes. John Walker Lynn, a white man would remember those days and understand what they mean on a global level. He read the *"Autobiography of Malcolm X"* and completely underwent a transformation.

## Turn Towards the East

Imam Wallace Deen Muhammad and Minister Louis Farrakhan played a significant role in helping people *turn towards the East* for prayer, and broadening their religious scope, especially after the departure of the Honorable Elijah Muhammad in 1975. This is the same year the *Raelian* Leader Rael, says he encountered a *UFO spacecraft* that told him about cloning and scientific development. Brigitte Boisselier, of Clonaid's chief executive, announced on CNN that "Eve" was born in the 21$^{st}$ Century. She admitted that her race was created through scientific means; Yacob's theory is starting to make sense to believers.

Muhammad Ali also travels worldwide teaching the principles of Islam. All three at one point were members of The Nation of Islam, a small sect that taught that the black man was "god," and the white man was Yacob's grafted "devil."

Imam Wallace Deen Muhammad distanced himself from his father's teachings and turned to orthodox Islam as practiced by Prophet Mohammed (PBUH) of 1500 years ago. Minister Farrakhan is starting to teach or emphasize that Master Wallace D. Fard Muhammad did not create the heavens and the earth. How could he be the creator if he was born in the 1800's and prayed to Allah during his lifetime? On October 20, 2002 he spoke on the humanness of the Nations of Islam's founder in his speech called "Surely Man Is Ungrateful." Removing religious superstition from a militant organization takes centuries to digest and must be done with a surgeon's hand. You would have to be a delicate surgeon to perform that type of successful operation in four decades. Minister Louis Farrakhan is doing the best he can to educate his followers about *the natural truth of Master Wallace D. Fard Muhammad*, a man who saw the potential of the black man to rule himself without the aid of European powers. Minister Farrakhan was doing a great job sharing the International teachings of Islam after the Million Man March, but then came the World Trade Center bombings. A crime allegedly committed by International Muslims. It must be painful to see your life's work severely damaged by lunatics on stolen planes.

## World Trade Center

That bombing almost destroyed the decent image of Islam that Minister Farrakhan presented on October 16, 1995. The bombing of the World Trade Center challenged all of our commitment to the American Dream and the Islamic experience. Those events are now considered essential to prove or measure our American patriotism and they are placed in the forefront of our minds, not as events that challenge our national legitimacy. From that time onward you are not allowed to have an opinion against the American Administration. We should be sad and disgusted when any person dies a violent death, nationally or internationally- Whether they die in the back alleys of Watts, or in the elevator of the World Trade Center. I simply ask you what makes you remember white tragedy over your own calamity? You would think that losing a member of your clan should have a greater impact on you, than seeing a member of another clan lose a loved one. In the black community the opposite laws of lose is expressed. We have more grief when white people die than we do when our young boys drop dead in the streets. This proves we are still brainwashed. I cried when those people died in the World Trade Center, and I also cried when President Bush started that asinine Crusade talk, because I knew what it meant.

## White Interest

I repeat, we feel more pain when white interest is at stake, than we do when young blacks die on street corners. We fail to recollect how many Africans have died over this battle of who will dominate the world! Nobody recalls the genocide in Southern Africa a little over a decade ago, where African bodies floated down a river like fallen leaves in November. Millions of people have died in Africa since that time and no tears are visible on your faces. In spite of these numerical disparities our dizzy minds will not let us forget the World Trade Center as speedily as we forget the Aids pandemic in Africa, or the Kenyan Bombings.

## 19 Men, a Masonic Number

Almost three thousand people lost their precious lives when planes hit special interest targets in Washington. D.C., New York, and Pennsylvania. These targets were symbolic of the brain, the strength, and the wealth of *the beastly system* ☠. I am aware that Americans will never fully recover after watching the World Trade Centers collapse on live television during the early hours of a *new day*. 19 men (a Masonic Number) would apparently change the course of history with box cutters and improvised missiles. I will never forget the humans jumping from the building while fire ate away the inner core of that monolithic masterpiece. The crackling sound of the building crumbling to the ground like burnt toast will never fully leave my brain. The scene left an indelible mark on my soul! I saw huge smoke-piles that crawled towards the heavens in an effort to comfort the ascending souls, and the lone helicopter that recorded the entire scene wanting to rescue the people, but was helpless to do so, because there was nowhere to land. Smoke leapt from the buildings like the aftermath of a volcanic eruption, forming the face of Satan, some believe.

## New World Order

September 11, 2001 only made us more fragile as a nation when it comes to the unseen and unpredictable terrorist. The four jet-style missile assaults against American finance and military would also be the pretext needed to justify Homeland Security and the solidification of the New World Order ☠. Special interest groups would win again, and the common people would descend deeper into slavery. Every act of violence against American people lends a hand to the suppression of American freedom. We lose twice when terrorist strike soft targets- these truculent acts are not just. We lose life; and we lose liberty. The so-called elite families' ☠ who instigate these wars care nothing about our son's and daughter's being zipped up in body bags.

The aftermath would be the icing on the cake that would erase your absolute freedom. *Population management* is at its peak post-911. It does not take much to terrorize us now.

We have the same tension level as a man on death row. We wonder if the terrorist will give us a reprieve or commute our sentence to life in total fear. Will the warden call our name today? Who will be placed on a gurney this morning and shipped to the local morgue over a fight they have nothing to do with? Innocent men and women being put to death for something the aristocracy ♟ started. Our nation has a feeling of being surrounded by enemies, and hungry financiers have made us a lot of enemies to worry about. The poor person who run around gunning for somebody never realizes that he is making someone else richer, and even his death does not bring the world closer to freedom, it does not change the power dynamics anywhere. American people have value in the minds of militants, of terrorists, of crazed gunman looking for another victim. Our Islamic brothers are fighting the wrong people. There is no justice in terrorism. You cannot reach your real enemy with a bullet. Learning to be self-sufficient is the weapon your enemy fears most!

## Xenophobic Foreigners

People who hate America think it logical to kill American people. But the same people, who ruled America yesterday, will rule it tomorrow. The real rulers of the world probably live outside the country. Knowledge is more powerful than the bullet. I will effectuate more awareness with this book than a man with an atomic bomb. Extremist from all sides will disagree with me; in their minds revenge is the gasoline that makes the world go around. They feel that retribution is the panacea to cure the world of social disease. Fundamentalists believe in matching force, fight fire with fire, eye for eye, one bullet, and one die. His or her belief system keeps everyone on edge. Everybody knows that more "soft targets" will have to die in the mind of the extremist. There is no way to protect you from a suicidal convert to a religious cause or a hawkish President with no balls.

## Police Car

The sniper waged war on America, and it had something to do with the way he views America. His personal experiences in America made him bitter. The years he consumed in the Army. He wanted us to feel his pain, his insecurity, and his hopelessness. His mind could not figure out how can a *man "fight for a country and come home a beggar."* This feeling created a delusional state that made him feel vulnerable. He wanted us to feel his vulnerability. Snipers have a way of making us feel just as vulnerable in urban areas, especially if he has a partner with a radio who can inform him on the logistics, or a police car that runs faster than ordinary cars. The more I look at this case the stranger it gets. What made the sniper end up in Washington D.C.? How did he become a killer in the first place?

## Encountering Snipers

September 11, 2001 exposed America's vulnerable infrastructure and its lack of airport security. October 2, 2002 uncovered law enforcement's inability to understand a determined killer or protect the public from sniper fire in urban areas. How did a sniper or snipers continue to escape the dragnet of law enforcement and destabilize an entire region? The military and law enforcement alike would have to go back to the drawing board, in hopes of improving the system of countering snipers in urban locales.

## Capital Punishment

Capital punishment opponents knew from the first time these crimes hit the airwaves that the Washington, D.C. sniper skirmish would hurt their cause and re-ignite the debate over the death penalty. Many people who were against Capital punishment yesterday will be for it tomorrow. This sniper spree would be the perfect case to argue for the death of violent murderers, especially those who kill multiple persons in criminal acts. I hope the sniper case will help all of us see how violence has gotten out of control. Maryland had a moratorium on the death penalty and many citizens now want it lifted. Hopefully, as human beings we will find a *'peaceful solution'* like the House of Yahweh is working on in Abilene, Texas.

## Ground Zero

A killer who can 'look down his sight and pull the trigger,' hitting his target every time. The sniper was someone who could *challenge, locate, identify, track* and *neutralize* an innocent person. The presumption was that an elite sniper outfit must have specially trained the sniper. There is evidence that the killers trained at a place called "Ground Zero" down south, according to newspaper reports. Ironically, the number 'Zero" was created by a Muslim long ago. Law enforcement regrets the media for calling the homicidal maniac a sniper. They feel that to be a sniper is a legit and honorable profession, not a talent to be abused or claimed by a mad criminal. Sniper or not, we must learn to figure out what makes these people tick! Snipers have lurked in America's unconscious since August 1, 1966, when Charles Whitman trekked to the top floor of the University of Texas, and created his own Tower of death. Mr. Whitman had some domestic problems too; I think he killed some of his family prior to climbing the stairs with his riffle and ammunition. Letters were left at his home explaining his level of stress in a complicated world. Just because he left a letter would not necessarily qualify him as a *signature killer.* America has been dealing with snipers for quite some time now. A sniper near a thoroughfare shot Dr. Martin Luther King Jr., and made his escape from a nearby hotel in a white vehicle. Three snipers shot President John F. Kennedy from a book depository, behind a fence, and some other undisclosed location, and walked and drove from the scene in a white Chevy, four-door vehicle. Leaders have always been vulnerable to such a cowardice assault. Psychologically, we have learnt how to block that fear from our minds. But why are white vehicles always involved in high-level assassinations?

## Military Veterans

Since it is our policy to ignore social conditions that manufacture maniacs, and promote schisms, more people will have to die at unpredictable times, in this American experience, because the dynamics of power will not change. In the Washington-area sniper situation 12 or more people would have been murdered as a consequence of a killing spree that allegedly escalated from a domestic separation. What is causing all these military veterans of the Gulf War, and the Afghanistan battle, to return home as civilian murderers? Did all of this carnage start over a domestic dispute or is something more sinister at work that your mind wouldn't even imagine? Why did the sniper continue to enter the infamous 'Skull and Bones' ☠ picture into the stolen laptop computer? I would love to track the medications all these killers may have used prior to their going berserk. There has been some evidence to suggest that many of the high school killings over the last decade were related to certain prescribed medications the killers had used prior to the massacres. Did the military treat John Allen

Muhammad before he left service with medication? If so, how can we find out what it was?

## Dreadfully Uninformed

The Skull and Bone ☠ at the top of this chapter represent the image found on the stolen laptop computer allegedly found in the suspects' 1990 Chevrolet Caprice. This symbol was mentioned on Geraldo Rivera's show on November 9, 2002. Geraldo Rivera is a quasi-Jew with the "Star of David" tattooed on his hand. If you connect the 13 stars on your dollar bill, it forms the Star of David. I would bet a million dollars, if I had it, on Geraldo having inside information on secret societies. It is believed that he belongs to a secret order and that his tattoo identifies his initiation ritual. When he made mention of the symbol found on the snipers laptop computer he played dreadfully uninformed. It was almost as if he was trying to simplify the matter. He acted as if he was hiding something. The quasi-Jew Geraldo Rivera knew what the symbol represented, but he also knows when to play dumb. A wise man knows when not to speak. Mr. Rivera kept emphasizing that the case against the suspects was "iron clad" and that the younger suspect was inpari delicto with John Allen Muhammad. I guess Geraldo was practicing objectivity in front of a world audience. Television should not be used to promote public opinion in cases that are going to trial, especially in cases where capital punishment is suggested and the accused do not have money to hire a defense.

## Inpari delicto

Inpari delicto is a legal term meaning both parties are equally at fault. In the sniper case all parties would be eligible for the death penalty. In a democracy you would think that media outlets would remain objective, but they cannot. A person can be found guilty of a crime before going to court with non-objective reporting. Members of secret societies know what line of reasoning they should follow and quasi-Jews influence all your major networks dramatically. Go out and do some research on "media monopoly" and names like David Sarnoff (founder of NBC), William S. Paley (head of CBS since 1928), and Leonard Goldenson (President of ABC) will come up repeatedly. In case you did not know it, their commonality is a quasi-Jewish ancestry. The glue of secret societies is big financial enterprises that are self-sustainable and quasi-Jews identify with this notion thoroughly. You are the ones that have nothing, and yet, you believe in everything.

## The Tomb

Skull and Bones ☠ is also a symbol of a secret society at Yale University. There is a popular belief in the so-called Sub-culture class "that the world is run by secret societies that clandestinely manipulate conflict around the globe for their benefit alone." They control all facets of currency, politics, and religion. You can find numerous books exposing different orders. Each *subordinate* order is connected to the Grand Lodge in England. What the English cannot control economically, America will manage militarily. And those who suffer from poverty and death can turn to the Vatican for spiritual salvation. The Vatican is an arm of the Octopus too. Either way, Caucasians remain in charge of every square inch of the globe – a vicious cycle that seems inescapable. Pat Robertson has a book on "The New World Order," which I recommend for those beginning to solve the riddle. Do not remain in his book too long, for you will fall into his trap of salvation. You may also want to read "Secrets of the Tomb" by Alexandra Robbins. Albert Pike sums up the mason's universal plan to diabolically rule the earth in his infamous book, "Morals and Dogma." "Order out of Chaos" seems to be their main goal.

People close to President George Bush are coming out explaining how "war hungry" the man is. General Colin Powell feels that the Bush Doctrine has placed him in a *"refrigerator."* An environment so cold, and devoid of humanity, that the General seems powerless to effectuate a warmer milieu. He is now a victim of the *"iceman's inheritance."* It is as if Mr. President wants to kill Saddam Hussein with the same megalomania, as Captain Ahab's desire to kill the white shark that he blamed for his conspicuous limp. You would think they were discussing a madman! Conscious people know that Mr. Bush is a high-ranking member of "Skull and Bones Society ☠." His father was *'raised'* in that same circle of intrigue. They love to fight for the British Empire. Mr. Bush is playing two roles just like Constantine (325.A.D). Constantine professed to be a Christian to the Roman people while maintaining his relationship with the Mithraic secret society of pagan worship.

## Global Conspiracy

Malcolm X was beginning to discuss the "International Combine" which formed exclusively for the benefit of Western Powers. He also mentioned how conditions worldwide needed changing, if conditions did not change, he predicted the fight for freedom and self-determination would reach the Western Hemisphere in a violent way. His explanation of the "International Combine" was vague because he only scratched the surface of the 'global conspiracy' with the little information he had available in his time. Had Malcolm X been alive today, he would have educated the public on the global order, which threatens to rush the world into a thermo-nuclear conflict.

The masses do not normally study bureaucratic systems even though these systems weld a tremendous amount of power over their lives. How many common men know of the Bilderbergs, the Knights of Malta, the Order of the Knights Templars, Council on Foreign Relations, or the Trilateral Commission? And yet, they can tell you the statistics on Michael Jordan's NBA record. 'Sport and play' is designed to keep you ignorant. Christian Ministers have not traditionally exposed the nature of the enemy, especially if the enemy was powerful. Instead, they do everything to protect the enemy and serve as a buffer between him and you. There is more to religion than meets the eye. All modern religions are studied and controlled by freemasonry. You can belong to any religion and still be a Mason. Generally, Preachers and Mason's will not reveal the secret to their congregation. At church this Sunday count the number of cars that have Masonic emblems on the back. The Honorable Elijah Muhammad amalgamated the enemy in one category and called them "devils." The bible tells you that the enemy comes to steal, kill, and destroy.

## Council of Foreign Relations

When a caller on a Washington D.C radio station question Rev. Jesse Jackson, several years ago, about the nature and purpose of the Council on Foreign Relations, he choked up and played stupid. Steve Cokely, a renowned freedom fighter, put pressure on Jesse during that same program to be more forthcoming and honest about "CFR," but Jesse dodged and ducked his way out of answering the original question. Jesse Jackson started ranting off about "black on black" violence, which had nothing to do with the original question. He even said that he, "Spoke at a meeting" of CFR, but "never really attended one." Jesse stated that the Council on Foreign Relations only makes recommendations, but does not make policy for the United States government. Today, we know that Jesse reported falsely:

> *The upper and upper-middle-class bias of interest group membership is compounded by the increasing important role that policy-planning organizations play in forming public policy. Some policy-planning organizations such as the Brookings Institution, Council on Foreign Relations, or the American Enterprise Institute; these organizations stimulate research and publish reports on major public problems and propose policy solutions to them.*
>
> *The use of policy-planning organizations is a major way for business interest to put their goals on the political agenda.*

> -Quote from "Empty Dreams Empty Pockets,"
> by John J. Harrigan

## Boule

With the 'war on terrorism' rapidly growing, all you hear about is the Council on Foreign Relations. And yet, Jesse Jackson would have us think they are not important to the political process. They play a significant role in the formation and application of administrative policy, at home and abroad. When the masses, or the grassroots people, want honest answers to what is occurring around the globe, we have to take the little resources available, and examine matters ourselves. No bourgeois (Boule) Negro is going to school you on the "Oath takers." How many poor people do you know receive "The Boule Journal?" Did you know that Ron Brown was a Boule who began to sympathize with African right before his plane went down overseas? Obviously, you can no longer trust the media to properly educate you on this subject or any other subject for that matter. As a high-school dropout I had to do my own research. There was no way I was going to allow the plutocratic media outlets to inoculate me with their half-truths and outright falsehoods.

## Adam Weishaupt

Attending small groups where indigent black men discuss "current events" as they relate to the European Union, Adam Weishaupt, Yahweh, Allah, God, Jehovah, Zeus, and deciphering what it means to poor people everywhere, woke me up.

## The Mosque

Visiting the local Nation of Islam mosque kept me thinking. If I felt myself losing my "morality and common sense" I would pay them a visit, or I attended some other conscious event in the area. I eat the fish and spit out the bones in all of these organizations. Purchasing cassette tapes on Elijah Muhammad, Malcolm X, and Minister Louis Farrakhan, among others, gave me mental life. During my attendance at the N.O.I. meetings' we were never taught to harm innocent people. "In the Nation of Islam you are taught to obey the law, and to do unto others' as you would have them do unto you."

## Supreme Wisdom

Even though I never officially joined the Lost and Found Tribe of Shabazz, I have studied their doctrine like a University Professor prepares papers for an examination. I probably would not know how to study if it wasn't for the voice of the late Malcolm X and Minister Louis Farrakhan when the later was resurrecting the Nation of Islam in 1984. John Allen Muhammad was familiar with some of these same teachings if he attended the Million-Man March or a few temples. However, if he only studied the doctrine for a few years, I assure you he was still a novice. It is absolutely impossible to get the *meat* of the "supreme wisdom" they offer black families in a few years. To fully appreciate 'the doctrine' takes a lifetime.

## Dr. Khalid Abdul Muhammad

In my travels I went to see and hear every conscious brother that spoke in Richmond from the late Dr. Khalid Abdul Muhammad to Professor James Small, they further provided me with the tools to see through the smokescreen and this enabled me "to think for myself." Steve Cokely is another revolutionary giant that is helping to awaken the sleeping giant and I pay close attention to Steve as a respected grass-roots commentator on exposing the Boule. I was in the audience at Virginia Commonwealth University, where students spoke with Kwame Ture telephonically right before his death. Brother Ture felt that the CIA poisoned him, according to his last statement on C-SPAN. Studying literature from the Pan-African movements as well as the New Black Panther Party kept me abreast with world affairs. Reading materials and books from Cheikh Anta Diop, Nelson Mandela, and Jawanza Kunjufu awakened a powerful self-love that is beyond description in the English language.

## Civilization Classes

When a man learns the true contribution his people made to civilization he becomes an upright man, not a sniper or suicide bomber. You cannot get this type of dialogue in Universities that are designed to make you dumb, deaf, and blind, and after four years send you home broke and psychologically damaged after being overly saturated with whiteology. You leave college owing thousands of dollars for learning about a subject that offers no usability in the real world. Name one job where algebra is used? I can honestly say it is a privilege that I was not Mis-educated in the "house of lies." Think about all the people who get out of college and go on crime sprees? Do you blame the Professor for their aberration or criminal act? No, because you know that human beings are free moral agents capable of choosing right over wrong. Moral choice is only affected when the brain is psychologically unstable or monetarily persuaded.

## Willie Lynch

Perhaps John Allen Muhammad should have stayed in The Nation of Islam a little longer. Or he should have joined some other conscious group like Kwame Ture kept telling people. "Organize, Organize, And Organize!" One of the snipers victims was very instrumental in helping to uplift African-Americans. It is a shame that his life was snuffed out by a crazed madman, who was probably a victim of the Willie Lynch theology, or a paid hit man working for a secret society. Mis-education is the main culprit for black violence in white America.

Something does not sound right about a former member of the Nation of Islam killing innocuous people. The Nation is raising people up, not putting them down.

John Allen Muhammad left the military after fifteen years and was no longer needed in mainstream America. What did he learn in the Military? He was taught how to kill, but no one questions that.

## Archons

Richmond is saturated and controlled by members of the *Boule*. Black Senators and lawyers are stationed in Richmond to *protect and preserve* the lies that keep the elite in charge. They are advisors to the king. If you want to properly understand the role they play, go back in history and study the 1710 practice of "*Meritorious Manumission.*" Dr. Claud Anderson's book "Black labor, White Wealth" will give you a precise definition of what "Meritorious Manumission" means. I can tell you that a select group of Negroes are getting rich off of your suffering. The men you see as *important and of influence* (archons) are just like Hayward Sheppard, the Negro who told that John Brown was about to attack the oppressive government at Harpers Ferry. They put your vital interest last so that the so-called elite men can be first.

Malcolm X came very close to uncovering the 'global elite' when he talked about the hotel where the Kennedy's met in New York, the Carlisle Hotel. Malcolm even mentioned that the Kennedy's owned the Hotel. History showed us how secret societies dealt with the Kennedy's. Elite assassins erased two, possibly three, Kennedy's off the planet for wanting to rid the world of Nuclear bombs, or at least lower its production rate. You would have to understand the Kennedy's connection to Ireland to fully appreciate what I am hinting at. Because of their Catholic allegiance to the Pope, the English crown never trusted the Kennedy's. They had to be minimized politically to prevent the Pope from having too much influence in South America. Malcolm X warned you of "The Big Six" when he criticized the March on Washington. All six were Boule. Go back and listen to his speech entitled "Message to the grassroots."

## English Crown

President George Bush, on the other hand, is well trusted by the English Crown. They have a common interest in petroleum oil and a common ancestry. They also want to capture land with high magnetic frequency poles, like Iraq. Little people are fighting and killing so that big people can get bigger. You must understand this first, if you want to know why people kill. John Douglas is famous for profiling the small time killers on the streets; revolutionaries profile the manufactures of killers lurking inside shadow governments. Collectively, we must listen to revolutionaries with more enthusiasm. Revolutionist will *"name the names"* of the enemy. "Psychology of Killing" will help you comprehend the mechanisms in place that influence murder on a global scale. Mechanisms like unemployment, embargoes, lead poisoning, false doctrines, deliberate congestion, unfair domestic relation's outcomes, exploitation, and other societal challenges that send people over the edge.

## The Rockefeller Family

The entire Bush Family is indebted to the Rockefeller's for an old favor. Senator Robert Bird, former Klue Klux Klansman of West Virginia loves to remind the President of who made him when they pace the corridors of the White House. The 'Rockefeller Family' owes their allegiance to the 'House of Rothschild.' I beg your pardon if you don't quite understand what any of this has to do with the Washington-area snipers. Before you finish this book you will see how the pieces fit together. Upon completion of this report you will know the forces that shaped John Allen Muhammad's mind. After reading this book you will never see the world the same again. A game is being played on the American people that promise to enslave us all within two years, if it works. Unsuspecting people are being transformed into walking time bombs. What role does our government play in manipulating violent events nationally and internationally? What role does our government play in making people sick so the pharmaceutical industries can benefit from your pain?

## Shadow Government

The government that you see out front, in the open, pays its allegiance to a *'shadow government'* that you know nothing of. Sounds like a script from a horror book. I implore you "to study to show yourself improved, not approved." Most of your *elected officials* are 33rd degree Masons. They have taken an *"oath"* to keep you in the dark as they manage the world in the *"Luciferian light."*

I have never seen or heard about a Boule helping a man from the destitute areas in which I lived. I did hear about Vernon Jordan working overtime to protect Mr. Clinton though. Vernon Jordan is a renowned Boule. Malachi Martin, the turncoat Jesuit wrote about the "Luciferian's" in his book "The Keys of This Blood." You have no clue about who is running this planet. And you definitely are kept in the dark on who picks your elected officials. You did not truly vote for them; they were handpicked for you. Have you ever wondered why the same people rule decade after decade, year in and year out? Have you ever thought about how many Millionaires are in the senate? Why are poor people left out of the democratic process? The best poor people can hope for is a seat on some local city council.

I took it upon myself to find out who truly rules the world? That democratic fiasco in Florida during the last Presidential election merely motivated me to look deeper. Al Gore is part of a secret society too, but the image they concocted for him is not hawkish enough to position them in the Middle East over the next two years. He will have to be used in another way. Maybe if the elite start to lose the 'war on terrorism' they will pull Al Gore out of the black hat like a white dove. It is all a big magic show.

## The Bilderbergers

I wanted to know the truth about "current events" and "actual facts" that shape the world. This book will share information with you that Dan, Peter, and Tom cannot share on their television stations. Besides, they also belong to a stream of secret societies that weld tremendous power. Ask Peter Jennings about his ties to the Bilderbergs and what role they play in International affairs? They meet annually at the Bilderberg Hotel with secret service officers keeping those uninvited guest away. As professional entrepreneurs they could enjoy a *one world monetary system*. For a poor man what does capital mean anyway? If you are poor in America you are poor in Spain too. This book will never make world news because it exposes the mythology of democracy and it goes to the root of criminal behavior.

On the surface Dan Rather and Peter Jennings mostly attend convocations that discuss economic opportunities for their colleagues. In short, the topic centers around, "what would it take for them to purchase the world?" Would it take a "war in the Middle East?" Would it take "a military base in Iraq and another one in Afghanistan?" They may discuss hypothetical scenarios at certain meetings that you are not privileged to attend.

However, subsidiary committees discuss *'mind control'* and *'demographic management.'* Yes, some groups strategize behind closed doors on how to completely regulate your and my life! Demographic management could include producing and investing in semi-automatic guns to be made accessible to inner city youth in hopes of lowering populations in high-risk areas. You do not have a clue what certain organizations discuss behind closed doors. Power is not as pretty as large homes make it seem. Many of those mansions are built off of your plight and inferior state of mind. Western powers are maintained by our lack of knowledge, not their abundance of wisdom.

## Dangerous Living

If "Skull and Bones" ☠ is in fact a living entity, what does it live off, how long has it been alive, and what does it want to accomplish? Better yet, what is its true nature? And if the Skull protects the brain and body, then where is the body and brain located? The answers to these questions may be danger-ous to know. But living in a world controlled by secret societies can be hellish anyway. Living in a world that is surreptitiously controlled by secret societies means that guns will be readily available; subsequently, so the frustrated youth can blow each other off the planet. *It means that television shows and video games will teach our children how to slaughter each other with precision and accuracy (One Shot, One kill).* It means that the pharmaceutical industry will continue to release information on narcotics so our beloved families will anesthetize them-selves from reality with cheap drugs. William H. Russell, the so-called founder of Skull and Bones (Baphomet societies) ☠ was responsible for opium distribution in America. Former President George Bush traded with drugs in Central America. You do not understand the mentality of cold-minded people. It also means that so-called Third World countries will be ultimately destroyed and eviscerated. You tell me what in the hell does pharmaceutical industries have to do with Homeland Security? There is a clause in the Homeland Security Act that concerns some people.

I heard on the news (November 18, 2002) that the pharmaceutical industry will be exempt from penalty if people die or get damaged from vaccination, probably related to the *'one shot'* they are planning to inject in every American. Somewhere in the Homeland Security Act is a *'clause'* to protect the pharmaceutical agents if you die from something they produce and place inside of you.

### 'God of Light'

You do not understand the evil spirits, which walk the halls of the White House, cloaked in mystery, worshipping the pagan "god of light." Those are the same spirits that placed cameras in your city to spy on you. At what point does the cameras' step across legal bounds and violate your and my *constitutional rights*? Admiral John Poindexter can answer that! How did the "probably cause" protection become obsolete right before our eyes? Notorious crimes and terrorism are used to justify your lose of freedom.

U.S. Attorney General John Ashcroft recommended expanding the FBI's powers to combat terrorism and crime in wake of the bombing of the World Trade Center on September 11, 2001. Common men do not know of Mr. Ashcroft's endorsement of *'Southern Partisan,'* a white nationalist group that has a long history of promoting bigotry and loathes at the idea of an *'egalitarian society'* where power is shared with so-called Negroes. They believe Anglo-Saxon men of European stock must only control civilization. If you are not of that stock I assure you that you are being used in some way to protect their vital interest. Can you hear me now?

## League of the South

The *League of the South* wants to overturn the 14th Amendment to the Constitution. If you are wondering who the *Southern Partisans* are, I can tell you that they are the children of the old *White Citizens Council*, the principal organization that fought violently against the *civil rights movement.*

You tell me why the Federal Appellate Court had to meet in secret to approve Mr. Ashcroft's recommendation on November 18, 2002? Conservatives use cases like the sniper to justify spying on the American people. Where were these conservatives when John Wayne Gacy was clowning around in the basement of his house? Where were they when Charles Manson was claiming to be "god?" Where were they when Beneto Mussolini was gasing Ethopians? They were locked behind closed doors preparing Former President George W. Bush's famous speech "announcing the conception of a New World Order." They have a diabolical plan to tighten the bundle of rods making many nations into one huge conglomerate, or corporation (E pluribus Unum).

You and I have been cursed with the privilege of witnessing our own loss of freedom. Your and my lack of knowledge will be the reason for our destruction. In the end we will all be "Skull and Bones" if we don't act now! And I am not talking about the skeleton that walks around in Tombs. I warn you not to continue being victims to the "idiot box," that is programmed to give you a false vision of reality. I am not suggesting that society should exempt criminals from punishment. I am implying that it is our responsibility, as human beings, to monitor those secret societies, government officials, and special interest groups that create situations that produce maladjusted individuals in the first place. You should also study the similarities of the sniper case and the Kennedy and King assassination. On the next page you will see the infamous anagram that I have been writing about. It will shock you if you are a thinker.

## Warning: The Anagram Exposed

The author believes that the intended victim of the sniper was revealed through an anagram on October 7, 2002. I have already discussed the importance of the date. Rearranging the letters in the name Benjamin Tasker Middle School will reveal the truth. Arrows will indicate which letters are to be placed where. We must condition ourselves to look beyond the obvious. You must first turn the two "m" upside down to form two "w." You will be shocked to see what becomes visible. Perhaps, I have decoded some classified information. **WHO** knows!

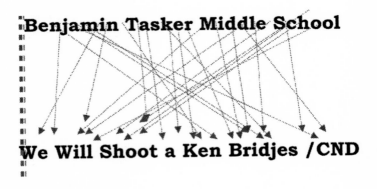

**Benjamin Tasker Middle School**

**We Will Shoot a Ken Bridjes /CND**

The only three letters that are left are **C**, **N**, and **D**. The author thinks they stand for **_Destroy_** and **_Neutralize_** under the **_Cointelpro_** program. The letter J has the G sound. Four days later Kenneth H. Bridges was dead. That may be the reason five stars were on the sheet of paper. You count one star as seen on the map when you draw lines where the killings took place in October, and then you take the remaining stars on the paper to mean each day the sun rises. That would leave four days before the actual crime takes place. I suggest that you go back and re-read the *Cointelpro* memoranda where they wrote about *neutralizing* and *destroying* a black messiah. Kenneth H. Bridges was working on liberating us economically. That would qualify him as a black messiah. His location was discovered by the use of a cell phone on the day of his death. He called his wife and told her not to worry because he would be traveling down route 1 right before he was shot. Cell phones have a microchip that gives your location in real time. If you still take this book lightly then I suspect that you are comatose. All the arrows point to conspiracy. I have been gifted by Yahweh to know and see certain things. A spiritual battle is about to take place right before your very eyes. You really need to figure out why Brother Ken was murdered at an Exxon gas station and why the killers called from an Exxon station. The secret societies really believe they have a "right" to rule over you, by any means necessary. I simply do not have the time or resources to figure out any anagrams connected to the others who were killed. Is it possible that the killer was sending a cryptic message to whoever was financing the criminal acts? You may right me off as crazy but the anagram should have you thinking.

# BIG BROTHER

The few who knew the reputation of Richmond's police force surmised that the killer would be captured if they approached Virginia's capitol. Upon apprehension the ultimate penalty would be proscribed. *Big Brother* is fully employed in this region of the United States. Satellite surveillance is secretly taped daily and only select entities have access to the highly confidential information. Thirteen satellites work globally to unify espionage for the C.I.A. Much of this equipment is being tested in Afghanistan as America hunts for Osama Bin Laden. Some of this equipment will be used in Iraq in search of weapons of mass destruction.

## Military Industrial Complex

The *Military Industrial Complex* calls their spy system *"The Beast."* America's beastly computer is connected to Brussels, Belgium. Dr. Hanrick Elderman, Chief Analyst of the Common Market Confederacy, revealed the computer in Brussels, Belgium in 1974. At that meeting Dr. Elderman "pointed out that by using three entries of six digits, every person on earth would be given a distinct credit card number." He called the computer, "The Beast."  Every human being that has a social security number is numerically coded in that computer for identification purposes. Your voice is already programmed in the computer for quick identification.

Your shopping habits are recorded through the extra-value customer identification card at your local grocery store. If you have a telephone, or have ever talked on a phone, your voice is stored in a database and everything you say on the phone is monitored. There are certain sensitive words that turn on the recorder in the computer once uttered over the phone. Your vehicle, cell phone, and driver's license have digitized marks in your digitized photograph, to monitor every step you take on earth.  Your teeth are registered in a centralized database for easy identification upon death. How do you think at 'census time' they come to your house and say, "Mr. such-and-such, you forgot to do your census application?" How do they know who you are if they don't know who you are? Right, they already know everything about you, your mother, and your cousin's nephew. I suggest that you learn how to decipher the *'Babylonian Numerical Chart.'*

## Ted Bundy

This volume will inject some controversial ideas into the public debate over what shapes the mind of a killer. One forensic psychiatric expert said that "Theodore Robert Bundy" killed because he hated everything that society stood for." Common people would not know that he killed three sorority women at Florida State University after escaping from jail awaiting trial for a series of murders. Once out, he broke into the Chi Omega Sorority House and murdered three women. My question to you is how did he manage to escape? The address to the Chi Omega dorm was 661. Religious scholars know the significance of that number. It has relations to the number 666. Again, how could a serial killer escape from jail in the first place? Was he allowed to escape after being programmed to carry out a mission? Was he let out to administer another dose of fear into the public mind?

With all the sophisticated security in prison these days, it is not stopping multiple escapes from maximum-security institutions. At certain times of the year the psychiatric industry allows selected individuals out of their facilities to insure federal funding. The recently released sociopath kills and rapes a few people and funding is almost guaranteed for the next fiscal year by local politicians. "If we had more funding we could have kept Mr. Blair a few more years and our community would be safer." You hear this same lame argument right before election time. If the murder rate starts to decrease in a certain locale, simply free members of a rival gang. This is what is going on in Los Angeles right now. Law enforcement knew how to break the truce, and we get tricked every time. Within a week the death toll will skyrocket. But who would think of a government that manages chaos by inserting psychosis into the equation?

## Predators

The public wonders why predators are let out of jails and asylums during election time. They have no clue of "The

Beast" who is calling the shots. A mysterious computer that instructs the Parole Boards on who should, and who should not be released at what time has your answer. Yes, a computer determines who should be let out. Certain indicators are programmed into the computer and the computer responds accordingly. When the economy starts its cyclical decline manipulate a war or let a killer out of jail. Now let us return to 'the nature of the beast.'

## The Beast

Imagine a religious fanatic trying to elucidate why America and Belgium names it's most advanced surveillance machine 'The Beast?' Those who make literal interpretations of the Bible or Koran may become concerned when Super-powers and her sycophants use 'beastly' appellations to describe its apparatus-calling its unmanned aircraft "The Predator." To use animal phrases in describing ones nature is somewhat arrogant. It is like asking, "Who can wage war against the beastly system?" Christian fundamentalist and Militant Muslims alike would take offense at, and be suspicious of, a Nation-State that allows such terminology. In the Book of Revelation the term 'Beast' is used when referring to the end times. Many Bible scholars think it is referring to the brutality such a government could inflict on its subjects when their policies are rejected. The United Nations is the right arm of the illuminati and they will pass any Resolution to cement its longevity. You really need to think about Europeans assigning themselves the right to disarm sovereign nations. Iraq's people will soon understand this principal as U.N. inspector Hans Blix and Mohamed ElBaradei of the International Atomic Energy Agency search for Weapons of Mass Destruction. If they are simply looking for Weapons of Mass Destruction they should start in France, England, Israel, Russia, India, Pakistan, China, America, and

North Korea. No one said anything when Israel gave Apart-heid-South Africa the Nuclear Bomb. Why didn't the United Nations send inspectors down there? Because the bomb was in the white man's hand! The Islamic world does not trust the "United Caucasians of the Confederation" enough to disarm themselves. Muslims know what Caucasians did to the natives of North America once they disarmed. If history is the best teacher, then you know what will eventually happen to so-called Mohammedans. They will become "ponds in the games" of white supremacy. Once their usability runs out they will be eliminated or contained. Even if this is not the white man's plan, history makes him suspect. The white man uses every bodies history against them, but they shudder when you point the finger at their ugly pass. No nation has killed more civilians than the United States in recorded history.

## Sebastomania

Would you trust a nation that calls itself a beast? How will Muslims respond if they find out that their enemy calls itself a "Beast?" If Sebastomania (religious insanity) sets in a person believing and knowing such a fact, he may take matters into his own hands. He or she may feel that whatever actions taken on their part, is justified if it exposes certain aspects of the evil government. In psychological terms he or she may be suffer-ing from extreme dyssocial-psychosis. The fanatical Muslim may fear genetic annihilation and strike out violently! His fear of death causes him to run full speed on a self-destructive path. In this case, killing a few innocent people to expose 'The Beast' may be his ultimate sacrifice, and in his mind, necessary. You can see how Muslims justify calling those who control beastly institutions "Apes and pigs." If you are giving yourself animal names, perhaps you only believe in *"Darwin's Natural Selection Theory."* What do you hold to be more important, *natural law or constitutional law?* Survival of the fittest in the twenty-first century spells "Mass Destruction." When I personally watch National Geographic Society every "Beast" I see is preparing to eat something in a violent way, masticating its prey with no shame, then planning for the next victim.

## Mind Hunter

Read the "Mind Hunter" by John Douglas and Mark Olshaker, they have an informative chapter on "Inside the mind of a killer," and they compare killers to "beast." Now that you understand the intrinsic nature of a beast, why do you think America calls her system "The Beast?" Is it just an innocent name, or are they preparing to kill millions? You may think I am brave for writing this book, or foolish for writing about what I know, but I do not fear any man. If this is truly a free Country I should be able to write this book without repercussions. Time will tell whether we have freedom of speech. If the government tries to detain me for some trumped up criminal offense you know it was an orchestrated trap to keep my mouth shut. They do not want you to know that the same satellite imagery and aerial photography equipment being used to disarm Saddam today will be used on you tomorrow. Is it true that the Pentagon secretly watched the sniper kill people from space, but never turned the tapes over to law enforcement? Instead, did they use the photo imagery of the Washington-area to study population movement in times of crisis? Right to this day the Pentagon will not release information on John Allen Muhammad. It is a shame that the new Homeland Security Act gives the Pentagon the power to house information on every American family, and they swore to secrecy that this information would be kept from you. I think Admiral John Poindexter appreciates his post. Your fear of terrorism precludes you from realizing what this means. Out of anxiety you are allowing Adolf Hitler to be resurrected as Attorney General John Ashcroft, George Bush, and John Poindexter. Wake up you fearful nation! They tell me the Tomb at Yale University has relics that belonged to Hitler and that these artifacts give them special powers. You never know what type of blood someone has until you expose the flesh and examine the contents. Your rush to judgment in the sniper case makes you miss vital information.

## Big Brother

Think about this when examining the indoctrination of the sniper suspects. A person can be programmed to accept almost anything. Yes, Big Brother is programming you right now! The snipers were stopped several times and let go even after an all points bulletin was issued giving a clear description of their car. I repeat, is it possible that the Pentagon was watching them the entire time, allowing them to terrorize an entire region for the good of the New World Order? What do you think a government would do to justify increasing a police force and solidifying a police state? You do not have a clue!

## George Orwell

When Eric Arthur Blair wrote his famous book "1984," using the pseudonym George Orwell, he could have easily been writing about Richmond, Virginia in October 2002. The sniper or snipers probably would have been videotaped loading the rifle in Richmond had they entered the city. Cameras are stationed at each entrance to the city and on many of the Boulevards and main thoroughfares. The Richmond Times-Dispatch wrote an article about cameras at the intersections several years ago. Psychologist and behavioral scientist can see how 'paranoia' can develop in the minds of human beings as society undergoes an obtrusive transformation.

Perhaps it is too risky trying to figure out the mental mindset of a vicious killer. The diagnosis might tell us something about ourselves. It might reveal to us the part we unconsciously play in shaping psychopaths. Robert K. Ressler should do a profile on the psychological make-up of President George Bush. What type of mind would make a man think he has the right to rule the world? Would he have to be arrogant and self-absorbed? Of course, Mr. Ressler would not get paid for exposing the mental state of the *initiated few.* In fact, they would probably erase him off the earth like they did many of William Jefferson Clinton's close associates. Read the "Clinton Chronicles" for more information on the "Psychology of Killing" among the so-called elite class. Forensic psychiatrists know to study and expose individuals, not secret societies that help form the mental state of individuals.

## HR-666

*Big Brother"*is a term used that was taken from George Orwell's famous book "1984." It is a euphemism for police state, paternal dictatorship, and loses of privacy for every person under the totalitarian regime. On November 10, 2002 it was admitted that the Pentagon is currently working on a 'computer' that will exercise unlimited powers to spy on citizens 'without probable cause.' Read HR-666 on 'Searches and Seizure,' and 'objectionable belief.' Groups in the Sub-Culture feel that this idea is manifested in the Bush Doctrine. We know that "The Bush Family" also has strong ties with Skull and Bones. Ms. Alexandra Robbins, a member of a secret society recently wrote a book entitle "Secrets of the Tomb." I doubt if she will expose anything of substance about the order.

'666' has esoteric meaning for the elect few. This number goes back to the ancient practice of astrology, or sky worship. Nimrod wore an amulet with mysterious numbers on them whenever he instructed his soldiers. Numbers had something to do with "The All-seeing Eye." I do not have the space or resources to cover this topic at this time.

## Bohemian Societies

Blacks in the lower economic stratums of North America are learning how Boule members report to the King (Layer upon layer and circle within circle). They have the complete trust of the reptilian government. They are the same Negroes who ran to master and warned him of slave revolts. They suffer from a psychological sickness called "meritorious manumission." It does not make one feel secure when you discover that secret societies are running your life in a sinister way. John Allen Muhammad knew of the Boule, the Bavarian order, and the Bohemian societies if he ever was around conscious brothers in his travels. These organizations are the "all-seeing eyes of big brother." Civil liberties advocates are very concerned about how "big brother" will affect the CONSTITU-TIONAL RIGTHS of citizens. If John ever studied among conscious brothers, like the Nation of Islam he would have to know something about all of the above.

## Ancient Babylon

Our century is metamorphosizing at rapid speed and too many people are being left behind. It reminds one of *Ancient Babylon* with the hundreds of stone lions at the gates to the city, feline eyes peering at visitors, designed to make one feel watched at all times. These cameras serve to protect private property on the fringes of the city, not lives in the inner city.

They serve to control commerce, not stop violence. Sadly enough, terrorists do not care about being seen on film after the fact. Mohammed Atta was seen on video-surveillance hours before piloting a plane into the World Trade Center. There was no way the video-surveillance camera that taped him for Big Brother could have stopped his assault on American finances, its military, and citizens. Simple methodology always outsmarts high-tech machinery. William H. Whythe, in his 1957 book entitled "The Organization Man" wrote about the world progressing towards a *"dehumanized collective."* A quote from page 34 of his book reads…

> *"And what a terrible world it would be! Hell is no less hell for being antiseptic. In 1984 of Big Brother one would at least know whom the enemy was- a bunch of bad men who wanted power because they liked power.*
> *But the other kind of 1984 one would be **disarmed** for not knowing who the enemy was, and when the day of reckoning came the people on the other side of the table wouldn't be Big Brother's bad henchmen; they would be a mild-looking group of therapist who, like the Grand inquisitor, would be doing what they did to help you."*

Mr. Whythe is suggesting, perhaps unknowingly, that there will come a time when there will be some confusion on exactly "who the real enemy is, or who he is not." Some may consider me the enemy for analyzing the killer from a sub-culturists perspective.

## Photo-Imagery

In 1957, Mr. William H. Whythe could not have known of the advancements in computer technology and its "infringement applications," using digitized photo-imagery and sophisticated data collection. In the conclusion of his book he intimates that 'individuals' are more powerful than governmental intrusion or organizations. We have the right and the power to change governments. It is supposed to be our constitutional right to speak out. I write about what I feel and see. This causes anguish in some people; other people express their conclusions differently. Fear cannot cripple my voice. Through words I will live forever.

# ESOTERIC KILLERS

In Erich Fromm's book "Escape from Freedom" he writes about mans feeling of isolation and powerlessness. These anxieties are real in the general population, especially these days. There is a whole field of literature on industrial psychology that spells out how man can become extremely disheartened in a society so complex. When anxieties increase in certain people they snap out. Their brain does not seem to be mature enough to deal with trepidation in a constructive way. The brain cells become entangled and psychosis takes root. Certain foods and medications can induce a state of demolition in individuals with specific blood types. When functional psychoses set in the subject will take every challenge personally. Although their brain is somewhat immature when dealing with conflict, they may be very intelligent in other ways. Since they do not have the coping skills to deal with internal conflict, they create a more horrific conflict outside of themselves. It is uniquely a diversionary psychology- forcing the brain to concentrate on transferring the internal pain outward. This methodology is designed symbolically to allow them to remove the anxiety from themselves and place it inside someone else.

## Cooling Off

The snipers mastered the diversionary anxiety technique in the Washington-area murders. The need for anxiety-trans-ference increases after each slaying. Psychologist term this a "cooling off" period. The Washington-area snipers built up such a powerful anxiety-stricken relationship that thrived off transferring horror into other human beings and society at large.

John Allen Muhammad learned how to transfer his fear in the Persian Gulf War. Transferable fear means someone will die or get hurt for the fear he feels internally. He drove up and down the Highway of death in Kuwait, a place where body parts were piled up to the horse's neck. Sub- consciously, this is why most of his murders were done next to the Interstate or highways. After witnessing all those deaths in Kuwait killing was second nature, it became easy. But killing was not enough in his infantile mind. He had to watch the news broadcast in order to reenergize his mental void and hype him up for the next killing. Since the slayings were done from a distance the intervals between killings became more pronounced. If the slaughters were done in close proximity, it may have taken longer before the need to kill re-awoken, or resurrected in his mind.

## Infantile Stage

You can accurately label the 'esoteric killer' a parasite. His inadequate feeling causes him to destroy the society in which he lives. He suffers from a peculiar antisocial behavior disorder. It does not mean the killer does not know right from wrong, it means they lack self-control. When one is trapped in the infantile stage of human development he can not tolerate responsibility. These killers are not capable of making a rational decision- something is not wired right in their brain. But they do know that what they are doing is wrong. You would not hide in a bush, or tuck yourself in a boot; to shot from an unconcealed position if what you thought you were doing was right. You would simply stand out in the open, drinking a soda if you thought you were correct in your actions. You may feel justification, but not a sense of right. In a strange way the snipers felt justified. A baby crying for some milk also feels justified, never mind the fact that the howling hurts your ears.

I conclude that their thought process is 'infantile' and their emotions are 'apathetic.' Something in their upbringing caused them not to care about other people's feelings. After more information on John Allen Muhammad is made available to the public someone will do an echogram on his life and may find out what went wrong in his early development.

Their dependency on aid organizations in Washington State reveals their lack of self-determination and thriving skills. They felt very powerless and insignificant. They even needed someone to help them purchase a car. It reminds you of a teen-ager needing "Dad" to co-sign for a high school senior's first automobile. Why didn't they tell people what they were feeling? Infants do not communicate in long or complete sentences. There were times when they tried to give people clues, but the subtle hints were incomplete. Babies pull and try to put things in their month. They struggle to experience life through their mouths. The snipers struggled to give power to their "Oral" stage of development. "The oral-aggressive adult attempts to exploit others and is envious and aggressive in social relations," and this realization can help you understand the threats to the Montgomery Police Chief through brief missives last October.

## Freudian Slip

The Forensic psychologist working the case understood this 'infantile' need and moved quickly to open up lines of communication. Eventually a Freudian slip would reveal the snipers true identify. You can call it "criminal bonding." The experts started off cueing. The Chief of Montgomery County used "short, precise, and single words," matching the developmental stage of the sniper. I am giving my opinion of the sniper even though you may think I don't have the right to do so. I may not have a college degree, but I am intelligent enough to diagnose a subject. You are doing no different at the Behavioral Science Unit in Quantico, Virginia. You sit back and get paid 'big bucks' to speculate on the motives and reason's people go off. But when black people kill you never connect it to Post-Traumatic Slave-Disorder, or the perpetual infantile position white America keeps black people in. No, you ignore that kind of research. Criminal behavior can stem from psychological stress encouraged by severe economic frustration, social neglect, and white privilege.

Poor people are not supposed to have an opinion on public affairs without the approval of prestigious universities. You must either get approval to think opinionated from some Jesuit college or some other religious society.

Extremist groups, who fear the encroachment of mono-lithic organizations, like America's new Homeland Security Department:

*(Acronym: Helping the Occidental and the Mighty Elite Level a Negative Dominance over the globe, using Surveillance and Eavesdropping Computers; thereby establishing Ultimate Ruler-ship Internationally in Two Years).*

Many blacks that live on the edge, at the lower economic pyramid level, think that time is here now! You can say they feel desperate. During the Honorable Elijah Muhammad's time it was said, "A white man's heaven is a black man's hell." The title comes from a soul-wrenching song by the Honorable Minister Louis Farrakhan. As the white man's home becomes more and more secure, the so-called colored man's house will go up in flames, and become insecure. I would like to give you a simple demonstration of what I am referring too: Europe has come together financially and they have developed a uni-fied currency, The EURO. Islamic charitable organizations cannot even catch up with their oppressors because America is accusing them, or most of them, of being in place to finance terrorism. Salam AL-Marayati, the Executive Director of the Muslim public affairs Council, said that the government is operating a witch-hunt.

Africa is financially dependant on European trade and their dollar lacks value compared to their former colonizers dollar. Europe is pretty much a healthy nation today. Africa is dying at alarming rates from aids, famine, and wars. Those are just two examples of the disparity in healthcare, and the inequality of capital, that are involved when you compare "the current ruler with the ex-slave." Without justifying John Allen Muhammad's actions for waging war on "innocent people," can you at least see how this unfair disparity affected his thought processes? If that is asking too much of the American people at this critical time in history, can you see how he was not really sure "who the enemy was?" His insane vision and hostility made him point his riffle at everyone. Was he drunk with mental confusion as a result of not being able to see the real enemy? Did his lack of success enrage his mental outlook and destroy his insight? Obviously, the people he murdered had done nothing to him. They had never disrespected him, nor had they the slightest knowledge of his mental anguish. John Allen Muhammad must have suffered from a pathological condition where he senselessly imitated the words and actions of white serial killers; echopathy is the psychological definition of what I am elucidating. This is why the experts thought the killer was white. In World history pale creatures or governments kill to get their point across.

## Anglo-Saxon

America has created its own enemies with her ultra-materialistic lifestyle and paternal philosophical ideology that makes white men "god and white men want the world to submit to their leadership without grievances. John Allen Muhammad taunted the white man by calling himself "god." Ilene Wuornos taunted white men when she killed six of them along Interstate 95. Her mind convinced her that men ran over women and abused them throughout society. Killing men was like cleaning the earth of evil people to her. How did John Allen Muhammad view Skull and Bones? ☠ Did he believe that Secret Societies want to rule all of mankind, as if they were ordained to dictate world policy with a "pagan god," or an Anglo Master Plan?

If that is the case, American citizens do not deserve to die for the global elite's greed! The global elite's willingness to gain

Mastery over what occurs in the Middle East has nothing to do with innocent people who merely want to enjoy life. American citizens are just as victimized by Big Brother, as sovereign nations struggling for self-determination are victims of elitist power-hungry secret societies. No righteous Muslim has the right to kill innocent Americans. Conscious Americans are frustrated too, but we will never strike out against your Muslim brothers here in America. Have you thought about that? How can you wage war against the "invisible hand" that molds and shapes every decision in your life? From conception John Allen Muhammad was born in a white man's heaven. He was aware that becoming President was impossible for a black man in the United States of America. You can accuse me of defending a "mad man." Even though that is not the case! I must repeat that I do not condone any criminal act on John Allen Muhammad's part. He was absolutely wrong if he is guilty! My sympathy goes entirely to the victims of this rich man's war. I pain for every casualty of terrorism. I want to remind you not to forget that we were all victims of the Washington-area sniper. We are all victims of September 11, 2001. We are victims of the history of slavery worldwide and white rule. We are all victims of the slaughter of Native Americans, the dispossessing of Palestinians from their homeland, killing of quasi-Jews in Nazi Germany, and other inhumane treatment around the world. All of our connections to the past are destroying our present. Modern people are dying from past discrimination.

## A Free Society

However, in a free society, or a truly free society, analysis is welcomed from every quarter, not just the far right, or the weak left. There should be a time when opinions can come up the center aisle without retribution. Adolf Hitler was against "free speech." I hope that I am not criticized for trying to figure out the mind of a killer as it relates to his psychosocial need to feel worthy. Eventually the Homeland Security department will remove all citizen criticism of the administration and its overseas atrocities. "You are either with us or against us." These are powerful words from the same President who loves to send people to fight and die, but fears a little weaponless turkey on the table at a Thanksgiving holiday. Whatever the Bush Doctrine enforces in the next two years will have to be accepted or else. Anyone not agreeing with the Bush Doctrine will be classified as Anti-Americans.

## Joseph I. Lieberman

This kind of blanket classification is dangerous to Freedom loving people. Those who believe that the world is governed by a global Zionist conspiracy will accuse Senator Joseph I. Lieberman of exercising his quasi-Jewish privileges when he purposed merging the government's far-flung domestic security functions into one department, which passed in the House November 14, 2002. The President will sign it later.

## Larry Silverstein

It is amazing how your major departments is founded, suggested, or controlled by quasi-Jews, i.e., Allen Greenspan, a quasi-Jew over the Federal Reserve Banking System; Larry Silverstein, a quasi-Jew, and de facto owner of the collapsed World Trade Center for 99 years; Major Media Outlets are also controlled by quasi-Jews. Can you see how conspiracy theorist formulates the idea that the "Protocols of the Learned Elders of Zion" must be true?

Every American student should read "The Protocols" and compare it to those who weld power today. You may wonder what "The State of Israel" has to do with the mind of an American killer. In order to properly diagnose a client in any field of psychiatry, you must learn something about his environment, his experience, and the events that shaped his mindset. Psychoanalysis usually concentrates on the subject who is being examined. Sit the client down in a comfortable chair and reduce his tension level, hoping that he will trust you enough to reveal personal ambitions and fears. They overlook the fact that we now live in a *global village* where people are traumatized by what takes place in other parts of the world.

## Economic Frustration

In this New World Order there is not one forensic psychologist or sociologist willing to examine a client based on International stimuli. What are the internal and external forces that shape the mind of a killer? Today, killers stretch from Hebron to Fairfax County, Virginia, from Russia to Watts, and from Johannesburg to Pierre, South Dakota. Suicide bombings today cross gender lines; beautiful young ladies are putting explosives on just as easily as putting on make up. For the professional person studying the "Psychology of killing," it is not always an easy undertaking. Behavioral specialist may conclude different reasons for the viciousness of a killer, but you may suspect foul play if all the analysis came out to be the same. I offer a different perspective. My theory is based on enormous economic frustration and societal rejection. I have lived around angry men who have never felt part of the American dream. Racism and social classification has made it difficult for them to be totally accepted as men. Their families do not respect them because they lack sustainable power. Who really respects the odd job man who struggles to pay the bills? In the urban areas many of these men join street gangs for acceptance. In college they join Fraternities to be accepted. Other young men turn to drugs for comfort and it is also a weird way of covering their true feelings. Malcolm X mentioned this escape mechanism in his famous Playboy interview with the 33<sup>rd</sup> degree mason, Alex Haley in 1963.

Patrick Rogers, a black man who was executed for killing a policeman in Texas said, "When you do not feel that your life means anything, the lives of others seem just as unworthy." On the day of his execution he said, "I'll ask Allah for forgiveness and I bow to no man." Mr. Rogers voiced his "Address to the Nation" on a deathbed, letting white people know that he would never submit to white supremacy under any circumstances. Why is it that the white world will listen to black men seven minutes before administering a death sentence, but will ignore them every day of their life? This book will not be taken serious by the media. Initially, they will attempt to ignore it until you begin to purchase it by the millions.

## Destitute Criminals

The legal system views destitute criminals as worthless. The prosecutors always have more money to prove their case. "According to a report done for the State Bar of Texas, Patrick Rogers' case illustrates what happens in so many death penalty cases involving court appointed lawyers in Texas. The report cited:

A) *"A total lack of funds for representation of indigents."*

B) *"A problem recruiting qualified attorneys to fully represent the suspect.*

In the final analysis, the report ruled the findings to be "Desperate." The State of Texas paid a narrow-minded forensic psychiatrist or expert witness to tell the jury that Patrick Rogers "would kill again because he is a sociopath." This statement was made in front of a jury of eleven white men and one Hispanic person. His peers never judged him in a court of law. Am I suggesting that Mr. Rogers should not have been executed? No, I am suggesting that the outcome could have been different if the jury understood what made him apathetic. Later the American Psychiatric Association put the expert witness, Dr James Gregson out of their association because of his speculative reporting. Dr James Gregson testified for the State of Texas in over 100 death penalty cases and according to Special edition, MSNBC, he continued to testify in death penalty cases even after APA questioned his methods and put him out. He labels almost every killer a "sociopath who will kill again." Most so-called expert witnesses for the State never look at the root causes of mental rigidity and anguish that culminate in criminal activity. The systems that engender insanity in the masses are never questioned because traditional racism and class protect it from outside scrutiny. Lead poisoning has a deadly connection to criminal behavior, but the lead industry is financially too powerful to come under scrutiny by government officials who have stock and interest in the lead industry. Household products can affect the mind in a similar way. The pharmaceutical industry has pills that engender schizophrenia in the minds of men that the masses know nothing of. What were the previous medications John Allen Muhammad took over the last year? Obviously, his court appointed attorneys would not have the cash to investigate these matters. It would be interesting to trace his steps in the military over the last twenty years. Some think he went to Germany and trained with an elite military group. Of course, the government will not trace his steps that would be a violation of his civil rights. What was he really doing in Germany?

## Escobedo Rule

Civil Rights advocates are gearing up to question the constitutionality of using digitized technology against civilian populations. When the spying mechanisms are used against criminals we feel it is somewhat justified. I warn you that even criminal investigation must be careful not to infringe on the rights of deviants. The Miranda rights and the Escobedo Rule are supposed to protect certain legal rights. A free society would want every accused person to have rights that guarantee a fair and just hearing, especially when the crime is a capital offense.

Law-abiding citizens should watch the legal procedures to ensure that practices are not developing that would remove layers of your individual freedom. We must also question how media puts forth information that convinces us of the suspect's guilt before trial. This is a dangerous precedence. Our Criminal Justice System has not had a chance to operate fairly in the sniper case. Your rush to judgment is unwarranted.

## The Peoples Court

If we continue to ignore this flagrant violation, people will be going to prison for crimes they have not committed, and the media will be the judge, jury, and executioner. I suggest that you go back and read what occurred in Nazi Germany. Propaganda was given to "The Peoples Court" and regular people were sent to their doom for nothing. There is nothing wrong with the media learning more about a possible suspect, based on facts. However, they should steer clear of trying to convict the accused by revealing incriminating evidence to the public. Police who leak critical evidence to the media should be severely reprimanded, and if their trust continues to deteriorate, then they must be fired.

## The Captive Mind

There is not one American who could see the two accused snipers as innocent, not even myself. The media has helped to form my opinion of them already. That is not their (the media's) job. Most people would say, "The media does this for purely monetary reasons." I suggest that you read "The Captive Mind" by Czeslaw Milosz, copyright 1951. I also recommend that you do your own research on "Media and Thought Control in the Twenty-First Century." Something very interesting is taking place right before our eyes and we cannot see it. Think of how the Christian religion has brainwashed ex-slaves to think that white people are Jews and that coming to America was the best thing to occur for black people. By thinking such foolishness they also think that Israel is a nation-state sanctioned by God Almighty.

Christianity is seen daily on certain television stations and on Sunday it is forced down our throats on NBC, ABC, and CBS. So it does not surprise me to hear about alienated black men turning towards the East, and changing their names to Muhammad. What has Christianity done for the poor black man in the poor neighborhoods of North America? Absolutely nothing! Christian business men refuse to hire them for a respectable job, education is too expensive for them to go through college, and the prison system is the only place where they are welcomed. If the establishment does not repent of its internal racism and start to empower more so-called minorities, social scientist will tell you that things are only going to get worse. President George Bush could stop the world conflict today. All he has to do is repent for the usury that drove half the world into abject poverty! President George Bush won't repent because he thinks white people are "gods" gift to the world, a chosen people. However, the world is shocked to here that a black man considers himself to be a "god."

## Criminal Enterprise

Muslims think that Israel is an illegal CRIMINAL ENTER-PRISE founded for the sole purpose of dispossessing the Palestinian Arab people of their land and denying their inalienable rights to self-determination. In 1948 over 800,000 Arabs were driven out of Palestine. It is felt that Adolf Hitler's effort to destroy quasi-Jews was the pretext used to win sympathy for the Establishment of the CRIMINAL ENTERPRISE. The Fertile Crescent is strategically located to situate an ARMY FOR WORLD CONTROL. Christians do not know how Israel was put together in modern times. They use the King James Version Bible to justify Jewish rule in the region. However, orthodox Jews do not even believe in "Jesus Christ" as the anointed one. Read the last page of "The Protocols" for corroboration of the above statement. They view him as an "illegitimate child." As a result of John Allen Muhammad's experiences as an African-American did he sympathize with Arabs because White America has treated his people the same way as Arabs? He was wrong for killing people. But what made him kill? His sickness even forced him to kill a very conscious black man who was helping to free black people. How can one become so frustrated with the white man's beastly system that he takes his pain out on his own kind? Or was the killing of Kenneth H. Bridges the main motivation in the first place? We may never learn what John Allen Muhammad was thinking, just like Mohammed Atta took his secret to the grave on 911, now it is forever cloaked in mystery and hidden in debris.

## Theodore Herzl

I believe Mohammed Atta saw the World Trade Center as an arm of the Zionists Occupational Government (ZOG) in Israel promoted by Theodore Herzl. As a member of the "Nation of Islam" did John Allen Muhammad have a worldview or a global outlook? If he ever read "The Final Call" newspaper or "Muhammad Speaks publication," not only would he have a worldview on politics and globalization, but he would have a *superior education* on issues like "economic injustice, minority over-representation in confinement, how AIDS is devastating the African continent, and he would be versed on the Middle East Crisis." In a normal state of mind he would be well balanced with "*Supreme Wisdom.*"

## King Alfred Plan

If John Allen Muhammad was mentally displaced for whatever reason he may have deteriorated psychologically and decided to balance the scale himself. Why direct his anger towards civilians? What did the sniper see in his victims? His victims were probably symbolic of America's vulnerabilities. In his mind, each time he killed a civilian he pulled back a layer of the New World Order. Killing next to Interstates showed how the government will put into action the "*King Alfred Plan*" with *executive orders* from the President. *The King Alfred Plan* was a hypothetical plan to shut down black neighborhoods in case of National Emergency in the 1960's. Entire jurisdictions were shut down in 'eight minutes.'

## Multi-Jurisdictional Task Force

In the sniper case, several regions attempted to work together using *Multi-jurisdictional Task Force*s to implement the dragnet in hopes of catching the killer. Apparently, it did not work.

Or was it allowed not to work? Down in Louisiana earlier this year, John Allen Muhammad told someone that he was working for the Central Intelligence Agency. Get yourself a copy of Newsweek magazine, the November 4, 2002 issue. John tells a relative that he is working for a secret military unit.

Should his claim be investigated, or should it just be ignored? What was the significance of 223 bullets? There are so many questions. Did the sniper or snipers use 223-caliber bullets as a coded message revealing the address of 'Skull and Bones' at Yale University? A numerical anagram written backwards would read "322." There was a time when the allusion to "322" would cause members of '*the order*' to leave the room where the number was uttered or the phrase "Skull and Bones" was whispered. You can find more on this information in Alexandra Robbins new book, "Secrets of The Tomb." Every organization has secret phrases to warn the "trustworthy" that intruders were nearby. The Zodiac Killer used mysterious messages, signs, and symbols in an effort to communicate to law enforcement. His fight was against the establishment and his victims were '*collateral damage.*' The Washington-area sniper understood the powerful meaning of symbols. Who was he fighting though?

"Collateral damage" is a military phrase that became popular during the Persian Gulf War. John Allen Muhammad and Timothy McVeigh were taught that killing civilians during military operations is unavoidable. When Timothy McVeigh was asked about the dead children in the Oklahoma Bombing attack he called them "collateral damage." Dead bodies become '*ponds in the game*' of war. Quasi-revolutionaries condition themselves to think like the oppressor thinks. The oppressor drops bombs on villages, killing babies, elders, and paralytics; therefore, the esoteric killer feels obliged to "fight fire with fire." Author of "Psychology of Killing" do not condone, in any way, the actions of the snipers, or Timothy McVeigh, nor the actions of Islamic terrorists. These observations are merely speculations and opinions of the Authors profile of esoteric killers. The Author sympathizes with the victims and their families. In a unique way we are all victims of terror. I have a right to publish this book because it is my unique way of trying to make sense of a senseless world.

## Merciful God

In the usage of *Tarot Cards* he moved beyond the realm of the physical murder into the metaphysical branch of mystery. It is similar to sects declaring Holy Jihad. Osama bin Laden uses this formula when he sends cryptic messages quoting Holy Scripture. In the minds of the suicide bomber it transcends the actual killing. They totally ignore the fact that they are worshiping a merciful 'God.' 99 attributes in the Koran should cause one to love his neighbor. Their real neighbor on earth is substituted with 1000 fanciful virgins in some outlandish afterlife. They look forward to an afterlife medal. The prize transforms the evil act on earth into a glorious application to enter the kingdom of Allah. You cannot reason with people who think like this. Your biggest weapon against people who cogitate like this is love. Was the sniper an afterlife thinker? Did his personal struggles brainwash him into believing that this life was so worthless, that sending people to an afterlife was a compliment? You have read where cult members refuse medical treatment for their children, allowing them to die, thinking foolishly that 'God' would have it no other way.

John Allen Muhammad is probably familiar with J.E. Cirlot's "Dictionary of Symbols" published in 1962. He may have studied the Kabbalah and higher levels of Masonry. If so, he may have reached the "god realm" in his own mind. Does 'god' need permission to be god? No, god is an autonomous being which makes his own rules. Introducing "Tarot Cards" helped to reduce guilt in the killers' mind. It was a strange way of saying, "My actions are beyond myself and sanctioned by god, who I am." "Dear Mr. Policeman, I am god." Stating godhood translated into "I do not need permission to take a life." The killer wanted the Police Chief to know that he had the power to save life if his demands were met in a timely manner.

### Denise Nelson

Perhaps the killer was trying to get Universal approval for taking the lives of so many innocent humans. He was struggling to define himself.

This point of transformation was a declaration of elevation to 'god ship.' In his mind taking lives made him a 'god' over the dead and the living alike. As a disenfranchised black man he exercised his authority over Washington D.C. Washington D.C is the seat of white rule. This made him feel invincible. He was unable to leave this new orbit. The power he received from the Washington-area was orgasmic and satisfying. He was finally front-page news. The world was finally recognizing the deeds of an invisible man. European serial killer Denise Nelson wrote an informative psychological profile on Jeffrey Dahmer years ago, explaining the killers need to feel powerful. The criminal mind can convince itself of *proper morality* in the most dastardly of circumstances.

### Jeffrey Dahmer

Jeffrey Dahmer convinced himself that cannibalizing his victims made them part of himself. There is a spiritual component to his reasoning. As reprehensible as it may sound to so-called normal human beings, this practice is symbolically performed during Eucharistic rituals within the Catholic Church. The Sniper case will reveal the killers' esoteric motivations and paradoxes. Erich Fromm, in his book "Man for Himself" writes the nature of "man as either essentially good or essentially evil, but as being driven by two equally strong contradictory forces." Hopefully, we will discover what drove John Allen Muhammad to kill when his court date comes up.

## Theodore Kaczynski

The field of psychoanalysis must adapt itself to the unpredictable *esoteric killer* that will pop up, from time to time, fighting against modernity. The Unabomber's "Manifesto" should be studied thoroughly because he gives clarity to the definition of "esoteric killer." Their fight is against an unfair world. In their mind the world has no balance. Theodore Kaczynski lived in a self-imposed exile from modern society because he understood that modernity translate into *'lose of freedom.'* However bizarre his methodology for getting others to see his point was, with the struggle for world power today, you wonder if he was right, even though his crimes were very wrong.

## Heightened Awareness

The killer may have suffered from minor episodes of schizophrenia or Post-Traumatic Stress Disorder, and gained access to esoteric doctrines (like "The Protocols of the Learned Elders of Zion," elucidating conspiratorial policies practiced by his own government). Add to that the socio-economic conditions, like unemployment and failed relationships, or unsuccessful business enterprises. Merge the knowledge obtained from *heightened awareness* under prolonged periods of distress with his progressive deterioration socially and he may feel persecuted by enemies without, causing oddities in his behavior, like crime. Lack of proper nutrition can add to this delusional state. A person measures his worth by his value to the society he resides in. When the person feels like a social outcast a strong feeling of rejection reduces his self-worth. This mental state further deteriorates as social systems legalize his alienation. When the Courts make decisions over ones family, like legal orders keeping ones family separate from the outcast, a feeling of desperation can manifest.

### John Walker Lindh

When man does not feel himself to be an intrinsic part of his community he may adopt another community. Since Christianity is the main religion in the United States, many blacks that feel, live, and breathe social rejection and institutional racism turn to Islam for solace. Malcolm X converted to Islam while serving time in prison for the same reason. John Walker Lindh, the American Taliban member who is now serving 20 years for fighting against U.S-backed Northern Alliance forces in Afghanistan converted to Islam at age 16. After watching the 'Malcolm X' movie he became increasingly interested in Mecca, Saudi Arabia and the religious pilgrimage to cement his faith. How could a white American youth turn against his father's catholic faith, his mothers Buddhist belief, and his country of birth?

### Holy Jihad

It was his _heightened awareness_ from studying a different culture that opened his mind to America's foreign policy. Mr. Lindh's new allegiance was to Islam and his goal was to fight against the enemies of Islam (Holy Jihad). Although he never intended to fight directly against America, unfortunate circumstances around the world precipitated his march towards exactly that. The death of C.I.A officer John Michael Spann at Mazar-e Sharif did not help the image of Mr. Lindh. No one took into consideration his spiritual journey and linguistic educational pursuit. He was vilified as an enemy of America, plain and simple. The media did not put much emphasis on his studies of the Arabic language in Yemen, or his study of Islam in Pakistan. Mr. Lindh was disillusioned with America's racist ideology and economic monopoly over the world. Why else would he leave a comfortable suburban lifestyle to live in a poor desert? Heightened awareness was the motivation that caused him to divorce his country to fight a poor man's war.

## World Health Organization

That same type of motivation is what is causing white youth around the globe to protest meetings of the World Health Organization, the Counsel on Foreign Relations, Tri-lateral Commission, and the World Trade Organization. Young people are fed up with such evil practices. When this kind of frustration reaches extreme levels it produces people like Russell Weston, the man who killed the Federal Officer at the State Capitol Building. Mr. Weston felt that modern technology invaded his home. He also felt that the Clinton Administration was intrinsically evil. On a very minute level he also fits the category of the esoteric killer.

## Oligarchies

John Allen Muhammad was fighting against the monolithic structure of American Imperialism. The people that died, in his mind, was the easiest way to effectuate a change in the system. When the snipers demanded $10 million it was only *symbolic* of the devastation American Oligarchies inflict on innocent countries for oil, wealth, and power. His actions were a microcosmic example of what Super-powers do to little people. The author of "Psychology of Killing" in no way condones the killing of innocent people, he is merely writing his interpretation and opinion of what produces such anger and insanity in the minds of men. Your criticisms are welcome; but your analysis of this book is better appreciated. So-called intellectuals who graduate from prestigious Universities are afraid to write honestly about controversial issues. They are confined to acceptable ideas, misnomer "Political Correct" concepts.

Sylvia Abraham has a book out that explains the basic meaning of Tarot Cards. The thirteenth card also means "I will no longer work for you." Did John realize that he was being set up, and quit his assignment?

## Master Thinkers

Master thinkers are taught that magic is 'black and white,' and violence is good and bad. To the *esoteric killer* it just depends on what side you are willing to fight on. The esoteric killer usually joins a legitimate religious organization for purely spiritual reasons. His belief in the doctrine is so intense that he evolves his own ideology, thinking that his interpretation is more in-depth. This type of person does not stay in the faction long because the group has no ready-made-solutions to his personal problems. He needs a quick fix, not a long doctrine. He feels that his interpretation of the literature has better insight and represents the true meaning of the association. He leaves the pure teaching of the unit and spins downward. In his mind, he is the only one willing to make the ultimate sacrifice. His lack of *emotional intelligence* will not allow him to see that the world will continue to function in the same way, even after his sacrifice and demise. Thinking to himself that change can only be made by his effort alone, he embarks on a mission to capture the attention of the world. All the people in his immediate circle are looked upon as agents of the enemy; they are brainwashed and no longer important to his life's journey. Proof of his apathy towards those who are familiar with him is based upon his not thinking how his actions will affect those who care for him. In a selfish manner he goes out to effectuate change, not caring how many innocent people will suffer. In his life there is no room for family and friends. Friedrich Nietzsche said it best in his famous book "Thus Spoke Zarathustra" when he said, *"Thus live your life of obedience and war. What matters long life? What warrior wants to be spared?"* What is missing is the fact that warriors fight other armed warriors, not unarmed civilians. John Allen Muhammad is no warrior!

### Brute Force

He is no revolutionary; he is a foolish man. When you embark on a journey to wage war with the beast; you must use intelligence, not brute force. Dr. Martin Luther King. Jr. said, "The enemy is an expert at using violence." You see Dr. King's point when you hear President Bush talking about bringing his enemies head back to Washington in a box.

Mr. Kasi was asked on the day of his execution, "What did your actions change about U.S policy?" He said after giving it some thought, "nothing." Initially, his distorted thinking convinced him that murder would change something, but it did not. Usually, the esoteric killer tries to instigate a situation that will cause total panic and chaos, forcing society to move towards revolutionary conflict, and usher in a better society. They are thinking like antiquated Russian revolutionaries. New times cause for new struggles. Violence will not change a system that stockpiles *weapons of mass-destruction*; however, knowledge will force them to change as you become educated enough to expose their racist practices. *Esoteric killers feel justified.* They think it is the only prerequisite for governmental change. The plight of their struggle offers no alternative to violence. This is why Palestinian Youth take to the streets with rocks, fighting the well-armed Israeli Defense Forces. To the Arabs the land they are fighting over is sacred. What would the American government do if the natives starting demanding Arizona back? As part of their claim and right to the land they mention a religious connection from 2 thousand years ago. Would the government feel inclined to appease them? I do not think so! Well, this is how the Arabs feel. The so-called Jews that are now running the Knesset are not the original Jews (Hebrews) who lived in that land during Abraham's time here on earth. They are imposters. It can easily be proven using history as a guide. Blacks in America sympathize with the Arabs because we too, have been removed violently from our original land, uprooted and positioned in a strange land, and lost our right to self-determination. The only difference between them and us is our fear of challenging the white man's evil ways. The Washington-area sniper lost all fear. His years of pint-up frustration turned to outright anger. He did not give a fuck about Bush's elite military outfit, or the Pentagon's billion dollar spying apparatus. Two determined killers shut down the entire east coast. 19 men, on September 11, 2001 got the attention of the entire world. This is a new type of challenge. Military strategists call it asymmetric warfare. In layman terms it means "a poor man's war." When you see Stealth Bombers flying towards caves in Afghanistan you know it is "a poor man's war." The American administration is embarrassed on the one hand, and prideful on the other. And yet, they knew it was a matter of time before the poor man would demand equality, or tear down all false security.

Was the sniper or snipers thinking in the same way?

## Dear Mister Policeman

Why did they target innocent people if their complaint is against big brother, or the beast? This type of communication from the sniper should not be mislabeled as "signature kill-ing." I am referring to the tarot card and message left at Ben-jamin Tasker Middle School where the child was shot. "Dear Mr. Policeman, I am god." To the contrary, a better term would be "esoteric killing," a killer who struggles to make others see what he sees, and feels what he feels. A killer who feels his actions can bring about a better society. It is a dis-torted patriotism of unrealistic proportion and evidence that the killer is self-absorbed.

Timothy McVeigh and his co-defendant would also be classified as "esoteric killers." They felt that their actions could help the world at large fight against a wicked government. To them, losing privilege was just as horrifying as death itself. The thought that the government would confiscate their "gun" drove them mad! The Waco Incident was mind- troubling to Timothy McVeigh. Patrick Henry did not know it, but he was a proponent of esoteric killing. "Give me liberty, or give me death." Extremist only sees things one way. The fanatic cannot see the serpent's venom as a possible healing agent.

## John Allen Muhammad

And yet, the esoteric killer remains misunderstood by many. Eventually he goes to his grave and is slowly forgotten. What was John Allen Muhammad trying to say to the world? By all definitions the esoteric killer has a polio-economic motiva-tion to destroy. In his effort to communicate to the political power structure he loses his religion. Everything he is fighting against he becomes. You can say his action pulls him outside of himself. The very system he abhors causes him to mimic that which he hates. He accuses the system of stealing, and then he becomes a thief. He charges the system with being a vicious murderer, and then he kills innocent people. It is not an easy task trying to figure out the mind of an esoteric killer.

## Health Conscious

If in fact John Allen Muhammad is the sniper, as the powerful media has told us, what was his motive? In the biblical story "John the Baptist ate wild Honey and locusts." Wild Honey and Locusts are code words meaning he was "trained to keep the whole law of Yahweh." Did John Allen Muhammad think his actions would make him a forerunner to bring about a worldwide revolution? What was John Allen Muhammad's underlying principle for eating "honey and crackers?" The guy who helped him purchase the car said he was extremely health conscious. He allegedly was reading a book on what you should eat to live. Many Americans are turning to organic food. Did he have a distrust of the food industry or was it health consciousness? How can one be conscious about his own health and disregard everyone else's health? How can you understand the importance of life and longevity, and prematurely send people to the grave? When the sniper shot innocent people he was not thinking about their physical wellbeing. A killer is a very selfish person who functions on the animal level. It was unequivocally ethically wrong and immorally brutal! As a human being I could never defend or justify the taking of a human life. That is not, and should not be the message of this book. This book will discuss some controversial issues surrounding the sniper case. You have the right to disagree with my opinion of "what causes people to go off." But I would like for you to think about some of these possibilities. Arrogance keeps one from seeing life the way others may see it. As a black man I think I am an expert on being black in white America. Many blacks are afraid to express how they really feel. The consequences could be getting fired from your job. Losing your family due to social pressure, and economic frustration, as a result of losing your job, only makes one feel more insecure. These outcomes can turn into realities.

## Victimology

A wooded area has plenty of food for those skilled in survival tactics. John Allen Muhammad would have received basic survival tips while serving in the U.S military. He would know that vegetation is sometimes hidden but he would watch where the birds land. Humans can eat much of what animals eat and humans can eat animals too. You can eat roots, beans, and berries. Honey has the potential of lasting long periods of time, and the natural ingredients are kept intact. The propolis and pollen are good to eat. I am not referring to the synthetic honey in your grocery store. White militia groups are learning to be self-sufficient in this way. Perhaps John Allen Muhammad robbed liquor stores to finance his "War on America" and to feed his stomach. His strategic targets were people. In his mind, every American plays a pivotal role in supporting an evil empire, directly and indirectly. Therefore, he deemed them targets. He made himself a five-star General and John Lee Malvo was his Lieutenant.

Was he conditioned to wage war against '*the beast*' and he taught himself to live off herbs, insects, and other foods that make one self-sufficient? Adolf Hitler was a strict vegetarian.

## Symbionese Liberation Army

It appears that John Allen Muhammad, 41, and the younger suspect was acting alone. We want to believe they were part of some global network of terrorist, like Hezbollah (the party of Allah), or some other group that has a problem with America's foreign policy. Perhaps a small cell patterned after the Symbionese Liberation Army fighting the evils of capitalism. If that were the case they would not have been caught sleeping along some lonesome highway (Interstate 70). And they would not have robbed small businesses to finance their murderous trek across America. They would have had the support and funds to flee the country. Those who are supported by organized terrorist would conceal themselves in apartment complexes, storage facilities, and suburban homes, not in a parking lot off some dirt road. Their movements do not appear to be sophisticated. Their movements do seem haphazard and perplexing. The randomness of their crimes made it very difficult for authorities to apprehend them. And yet, there is no indication or substantiation that they had a political agenda. Nonetheless, we want to feel they were part of something huge. We want to think that these senseless acts have some meaningful connection. There is speculation that they had ties with the clumsy *Shoe Bomber* who had horrendous difficulty striking a match aboard an airplane. This possible association is supposed to be based on traveling, by all parties, at different times, to the Caribbean. This conjecture will never be substantiated. I suppose this is the Caribbean connection that can be used to get tough on Immigration. Haitians seeking political asylum would get the drift of what I am referring to. Dark-skinned immigrants are treated different from fair-complexioned immigrants. Conservatives arguing for more restrictions on America's boarders will use the "sniper case" to justify their rigidity. There will be a time when entering America, visitors will have to submit to microchip implants for monitoring and stationary reporting at regional locations spread about the states. Each visitor will be injected with the rice-size chip upon leaving his or her country. Terrorism will be the justification for imposing such a policy. The sniper case will also serve to erase some of our freedoms. Is this part of the Master Plan? Take advantage of every major criminal event that can support tougher restrictions on American citizens!

## Richard Reid

There is no way they, the snipers were acting single-handedly! They must be allied with some militant assembly. The same type of group that blows up Disco's in Indonesia, or planes over the ocean. Richard Reid had traveled frequently and studied the weaknesses of Airport security. Gayle River's wrote a book entitled "The War against the Terrorists," back in 1986. Mr. River's warned of the poor security at America's airports and he intimated that terror would strike the United States. He was worried about airline security procedures. Can America's enemies purchase his book? Of course, they can buy his book detailing breaches in security. Perhaps the sniper was someone who was trained well as a determined terrorist through reading local newspapers. The public library has enough information to instruct deranged and angry men on how to kill. It is believed that the snipers obtained detailed information that produce fatal toxicity. Now the question is what was the sniper or snipers motivation and where did the killer learn to murder. In Gwynne Dyer's book entitled "War" he writes about training a man to kill. He said a place like "Parris Island," when successful "can produce a soldier who will kill because it is his job." What type of training did John Allen Muhammad have? Was he ever trained like Richard Reid? What do you think John Allen Muhammad would say his role in terrorism is? I bet he would tell you that there is no global connection between him and terrorist. He would tell you that the Nation of Islam is totally against his criminal conduct and would never condone violence without the component of self-defense being present. In short, he probably acted alone. But the mystery of the anagram is very suspicious to me.

## Aimal Khan Kasi

His situation is unlike the Pakistani national, Aimal Khan Kasi, who killed two CIA employees in 1993. A week before his execution, November 13, 2002, at Greensville Correctional Center, Mr. Kasi told a local newspaper that his actions were "retaliation against U.S government" for their policy in the Middle East and its support of Israel. His death may have a domino effect around the globe. Unbelievably, Mr. Kasi did not agree with the terrorist who killed civilians in New York (World Trade Center) on September 11, 2002, even though he feels killing is necessary in the war against oppression. He feels that oppression is worse than slavery. Mr. Kasi directed his attack on specific governmental targets. In his mind government personnel is perfectly acceptable because it is their labor, which feeds the beast. He minimizes that type of murder to be a 'justifiable homicide.' Almost like an officer killing a rapist while in the line of duty. He apparently acted alone, but is seen as a hero in Islamic countries that dislike America's foreign policy. Mr. Kasi felt it was his duty to kill officials of the government. In fact, this would make him an esoteric killer. John Allen Muhammad and the younger suspect declared war on all Americans, if in fact they are the snipers. What would make a former member of the Nation of Islam act in such a bizarre way? White killers like Joseph C. Palczynski Jr., had a long criminal history that lasted 13 years. He killed four women. Domestic Violence was his biggest problem. He was shot to death while sleeping during a hostage siege in Baltimore, Maryland on March 21, 2000. Mr. Palczynski also had a history of mental problems for which he was confined in psychiatric institutions. The snipers would be caught sleeping too, with their guards down, at a rest stop off Interstate 70.

## Dion Terez

A rampage killer, Dion Terez shot three people on August 10, 1993 at a McDonald's restaurant after being fired from Motorola. He videotaped himself the night before the massacre. His actions and videotaped confession illustrates that cameras will never deter a determined criminal. Instead of directing his anger at the people who fired him, Tares went after innocent people. In his last testament he expressed how "life does not mean anything for individuals." Life was no longer purposeful. He admired the boldness and fearlessness of people like Jeffrey Dahmer and Adolf Hitler. His rampage was a symbolic gesture to express his problems with life, with women, jobs, his overall frustrations, and his inability to deal with these matters in a healthy way. Mr. Tares felt that society was crazy and hopeless. He was the only sane person so everyone else was worthy of death.

## The Psycho's Mind

In a similar way John Allen Muhammad's actions appear to come from social failure and economic frustration. Possibly even the lack of parental influence in his early development. This underestimated sense of self, as a consequence of poor nurturing, opens the door to all kinds of vices. Some humans cannot take abandonment and rejection. It causes their brain to become agitated. Megalomania sets in and they live to get revenge on somebody, anybody for this feeling. Yes, somebody means anybody in the psycho's mind. Killers are very sensitive people and their ultra-sensitivity distorts their thinking. They have a very primitive socialization. Emotionally they are developmentally infantile. People mistake their childish humor with pleasantness. The reality is that they are very jealous individuals who have a strong need to destroy what they do not understand. But there is something in their brain controlling their imaginations. Amygdale highjacking occurs regularly and they can snap out at any time. Certain medicines and foods can serve to manipulate this agitated state. Social pressures are the main stressors that cause them to go postal. It would be interesting to track everything that John Allen Muhammad ate over the last six years. They know right from wrong but psychologically they are not totally in control of their mental faculties. These mental inadequacies that I suspect John Allen Muhammad suffers from is what causes me to believe he acted alone, without the aid of terrorist. Yes, John had to be acting alone, according to the facts so far presented. Being alone was nothing new to John, he felt alone most of his life. The early lose of his mother and the subsequent lack of his fathers involvement primed him to have no feelings for, or respect of family. He felt different from everyone else.

## New Babylon

His case is a warning to the African-American male population that father participation is needed to stop the violence. We can no longer allow others to bring up our children. If we fail to raise our children, then someone else will. The younger suspect somehow was put in a situation where John Allen Muhammad served as a substitute father. This surrogate family decided to fight against the world, smash stability, declare war on America, and sabotage any trace of tranquility. New Babylon became their target.

# NEW BABYLON

We marvel at how many enemies *New Babylon* has! Why even Fundamentalist Christians call America the *New Babylon* that is mentioned in the Book of Revelation. *New Babylon* is prophesied to instigate and manipulate the war of Armageddon. This war will bring about destruction (devastation capable of ending all battles). It is also supposed to promote the *'Mark of the Beast.'* Why do Third-World countries consider America to be that system? Only a Superpower has the ability to institute and promote a system to control all systems. Only a Nuclear Power can pass a law that governs all nations. The Bush Doctrine wants to police and impose her "beastly system" on all of mankind. She wants to be the only nation in control of Weapons of Mass Destruction. In a fatherly way, she instructs developing countries to cease from wanting to be like daddy.

Only the parent can play with dangerous toys. Everyone, even Russia, must now cooperate with New Babylon. China and Northern Korea must get in line too, or else!

Weak nations can never bully strong nations to accept a *mark*, or *system*. Only a powerful nation can implement that *mark, or system* on a global level. And Muslims feel that the upcoming war in the Persian Gulf is designed to do just that. They feel that the United Nations is a puppet organization managed by *The Beast*. Militant Muslims see America as a *'perverted generation,'* the *Great Satan*. They shudder at the thought of America's pornography industry, liquor stores, crime rate, forbidden foods, and usury. What type of policy would *New Babylon* legislate to protect itself from her archenemy, the militant Muslims and those who dare to think different? What would she put in place to silence her critics?

Did John Allen Muhammad see America as a righteous Nation-State? Or did he see a racist kingdom designed to keep underdeveloped countries eternally behind industrial nations, nations that best serve Nimrod's children? Is America a global network of rich families, like Rockefellers and Bush's, who could care less about poverty-stricken countries where children die daily? What would be Muhammad's view of Allen Greenspan or Larry Silverstein? Would this confirm his suspicion of Jews as conspirators operating from the "Protocols of the Learned Elders of Zion?" His feelings may be identical to White Militia groups or Muslims who teach a similar doctrine of Jewish control of major institutions. The Protocols of the Learned Elders of Zion is being aired on Egyptian television and skeptics are complaining that it is anti-semantic. They feel it is a false doctrine written by Russian propagandist who wanted to discredit quasi-Jews. Knowledge in the hands of an angry man can be fatal.

Something in our psyche will not permit us to fathom two African-Americans acting alone, trying to kill as many citizens as possible in their own Country. Every one was in their line of fire to receive a fatal shot. So if you think the Jew or the white man is the enemy, why target blacks and Koreans? Remember that confusion has no particular order. It gyrates and spins, hitting everything in its path. It reminds one of tornado's that struck America in early November 2002.

What is the world coming to? Everyday now we are hearing about mass, spree, and serial killers. Persian Gulf veterans are murdering their wives. White children are going in schools and acing everybody in sight. In the United States of America the Teen suicide rates are rising alarmingly. Mexican railroad killers riding the tracks back and forth to America, killing people near the path of the train. No one feels safe anymore.

Pharmaceutical industries are getting richer selling anti-depressant drugs. Now black men are acting just as sadistic as their white counterpart. Even the suicide rate is moving upward in the African-American population. State and Federal prison's illustrate how many blacks get convicted for either selling poison to other blacks or taking lives of blacks. If I wrote about the mandatory sentencing practice that sends minorities to prison for long periods of time you would charge me with digression.

Killers represent the worse of our modern times, but to killers modern times represent the worse of all time. As a matter of fact, killers do not give a damn about your modernity! They travel a meandering path of pandemonium. They seek to destroy every reminder of modernity. Through violence, vandalism, and viciousness they attempt to journey back to primitive times. Once upon a time, when the only law was lawlessness, people hurt and murdered each other. A few poor blacks are taking this trip back through time, riding a bus driven by white folks previously.

It would cause us too much anguish to think that black men do not feel any connection to a Country that enslaved their ancestors and placed them perpetually beneath the white man before and after the signing of the emancipation proclamation. Of course, only a minority of black men feels this way, or reveals that they have such hostile feelings. John Allen Muhammad is probably one of the rare men who could care less if you knew the intensity of his hatred towards your world. Just like only a minority of whites expose how they feel about Negroes, or how they feel about *affirmative action*. If you don't ask they won't tell. How many brothers feel the fury? How many homeless and dejected brothers want to shoot you between the eyes? We must begin to think about this and address it straightforwardly and honestly. If you want a better society, then you must look at the worse things in your existing culture. America cannot afford to continue ignoring the plight of black men. We feel a tremendous sense of alienation. That alienation develops into rage.

Rage is something that builds up over a period of time, and then explodes! In its developing stages you cannot see it at all. It is like the colorless, odorless gas that killed those hostages and hostage takers in a theater this year. It germinates deep inside, taking on a life of its own. As it matures you notice little pockets of frustration exuding from the person it inhabits. Initially the irritation seems normal. But as support systems fail the agitated state goes haywire.

First, an angry response to a minor incident, then obnoxious words to a loved one, next the demonstration of violence towards the world you do not understand. Or perhaps you understand it all too well! Black men have learnt how to hold their rage in longer than their counterparts. It is a common occurrence for white men to go off and shoot up the workplace. In the minds of forensic scientist your serial killers are white men. In the sniper case the entire forensic specialist team was dead wrong. They thought the killer or killers were white. From previous cases it was always a Caucasian. You would hear statements like, "Oh, he could not take the pressure." Maybe you would hear that he lost his job. Black men have become immune to not finding jobs, not maintaining employment, and do not mention losing one.

Historically, black men were penalized severely for showing or expressing how they felt. During reconstruction black juveniles were hung for burning down barns in Richmond, Virginia. There was never a question of his age! The maximum penalty has always been enforced in the black community, so we have learned how to "lay low, or just be cool." Blacks were told to "stay in your place." Subsequently, our rage is hidden in our smile. It is tucked away smoothly beneath our tongue. We also hide it in our dress, our material possessions, and inside the lyrics of our song. We are reluctant to tell you how we feel. "What you say can and will be used against you." Brothers have heard this warning repeatedly while simply standing on a sidewalk. Besides, we do not really think you care how we feel as long as you are in charge. White men control the political system, Jews control the Federal Reserve Bank, white men control the Church, and education too, all controlled by someone other then blacks. This unbalanced economy produces rage.

When black men fail to exercise control over their own lives the 'wolf of justice' encircles them, and snatches away so-called privileges. Sometimes the law enforcers simply "kick their ass" like they did Rodney King a decade ago. What gives the white man the right to control every facet of the ex-slaves life? He gets this right from politics and the gun. He maintains it through subtle threats like "military response systems." The relationship is not balanced at all. The way the system is set up black men collectively cannot, or should I say, have not, been able to remove any privileges from white men when they are in violation. Example: What can black men do about Enron? Absolutely nothing! What can black men do when an actress, Winona Ryder, gets caught red-handed on video surveillance shoplifting and never goes to jail? Every shoplifter in the nation should get out of jail tonight. When the Criminal Justice System does work for black men, like O.J. Simpson white people complain that it is not fair. They never think about all the innocent brothers doing life for being in the wrong place at the wrong time, like political prisoner Mumia Abu-Jamal. Black men cannot even control what decisions the Courts make over his family. The ultimate decision will come from a group of white men. Some Judge told John Allen Muhammad that he was now inconsequential to the outcome of his family and that he could no longer exercise parental authority over his children, or play a pivotal role in their life. Perhaps he was a risk to his children, we don't know. Over the last few weeks I have not heard any reports from Child Protection Agencies reporting to authorities on his family situation before he decided to snap out. His children have not reported physical abuse, from what I have heard. Even if he contributed to the court disposition in regards to the divorce from his two wives, based on his negative behavior towards his family, it does not eradicate the fact that America took something from him before he was born. John Allen Muhammad was born a 'black boy.' I strongly recommend you read Richard Wright's famous book entitled "Black boy." John was born with limited power as a result of institutionalized racism. He was born a so-called second-class citizen, whatever that means. As a black boy he knew his place. It was a place of *subtle shame*. A place in his life where high-stress and distress reign supreme. A place where disgrace bubbled and turmoil reigned in the hearts of black men. The black man is shameful that his ancestors allowed the weakest race on earth, the European race, to conquer them without a conflagration. "How can so few of them rule so many of you? That is the question," according to Malcolm X," a famous debater and self-appointed Black Nationalist. In his, the black man's, subconscious mind they should have fought back, even if it meant death. Today Indians and Japanese are respected worldwide because they fought the beast back. John probably feels that Nat Turner should have done more damage to the enemies of freedom just like Senator Trent Lott felt that segregation was best for white America.

Maybe John Allen Muhammad would not be so angry if he had a chance, a real chance at becoming President of a nation his descendants served so faithfully. Not simply a ventriloquist like Condoleezza Rice or Colin Powell. If he had a genuine opportunity to be on an equal footing with Donald Trump, or William Gates, what would he be like? He realizes that the cards have been stacked against him. He did not want to play the game anymore and started sending the cards back. He did not send a Tarot card; he sent a Terror Card! You can see it towards the front of this book. In his mind Nat Turner should have murdered every slave master from Virginia to Spain. The pain resulting from being a number in a conquered ethnic group has a numbing affect on the soul. It transforms former slaves into tyrants. As this pain moves inward it transforms into a unique narcissistic Disorder. Did this cause John Allen Muhammad to snap out, or was his murder spree simply the outcome of the court case that took away his custodial rights as a man? I think it was the accumulation of all the above. George Lester Jackson mentioned some of these components in his famous book "Blood in My Eye." Comrade Jackson said "they won't count me among the broken men." When a man gets fed up with his condition all he sees is blood. His rage becomes an obsession. You can see it in his eyes. I see it everyday among ghetto youth. A look of "don't fuck with me, I'll kill you." It is this fixation that causes him to place bullets in his gun, or sharpen his knife. It is this fixation that discourages him from reading, going to school, or looking for a job (a job is known as "Slaving" to destitute Negroes). In his mind, someone has to pay for what he feels daily. It is not fair to him that people can go about their daily routine, smiling, profiting, exploiting, investing, and recreating while he suffers the pain of 400 years. He walks up and down Main Street looking into the faces of white men and black women, thinking that they are looking at him, and secretly thinking derogatory things about him. Paranoia sets in. He wants to cry out, "You all made me this way, you bastards." No one escapes his criticism. The black businessman is an "Uncle Tom" to him. And the corporate boss a "slave master." Both are guilty of benefiting from an oppressive regime that makes him feel awkward. The black preacher is a bigot, a faggot, and a liar. He thinks to himself, "How in the hell can Jesus be white and hide in Egypt among blacks?" Or, "If Africa was so bad, why did God send all the prophets there to learn the secrets of the Universe?" These are some of the contradictions the black man is faced with. The most painful paradox he fights inwardly against is the money owed to him from his ancestor's slavery. In his heart he feels that America is strong because he was made weak. Not of his own doing, of course, but as a result of historical servitude.

The fact is that our battle to receive *reparations* has been ignored. No one is listening to our cry for total equality. All we ever wanted from white men was a fair chance. We want an honest opportunity to compete equally among other men in a fair arena. Not one black man has had a fair chance in this society, not one. Michael Jordan, Tiger Woods, none of them can claim equality with the white man. They think they can. But you ask them who counts their money and that alone will settle it.

Many of us have built in rage that has festered over 400 years, the pain, and the anger transfixes a state of confusion in our mind, a mystification that drive us down the road that ends in self-destruction. Social scientist will tell you that whenever you disenfranchise a man from the benefits of a particular community he will no longer feel loyalty to that   population. Subconsciously, he may want that community to fall to pieces at its core, since it denies his humanity and suppresses his basic potential to make it to the top. He is aware that society owes him something so powerful, and yet, he knows the system will ignore its debts to him, while at the same time forcing him to breathe life into the very machine that destroyed his potential to rule his own kingdom. It will be demanded of him to pay taxes and assimilate into his oppressor's world. He will fight his oppressor's enemies for him, only to come home a broken man, not even respected by his loved ones. He feels like a fool. But he is not sure where the feeling comes from. You have just read some reasons why blacks from the grass-roots will doubt the total guilt of John Allen Muhammad. If he is guilty the system is still at fault. John Allen Muhammad is the creation of Americanization. Dr. Frankenstein, who was presumably a Jew, made the monster that eventually would kill him. Was the monster truly guilty of a Capital Offense, or was he acting in accordance with the rage his manufacturer produced within him?  America, I dare you to think about this in the eyes of your black subjects! Racism causes us to rationalize every accusation, deny all controversial facts about ourselves, about John, and argue against the logic put forth by white America. Are we embarrassed that the sniper was black? Yes, but we are also ashamed that he was an Americanized black man, clean-shaven, standing erect, intelligent, patriotic enough to fight for the Country, and with all this, he was still not able to find his place in white society. In short, racism has driven us mad and he showed us how crazy it can make us! Now we want to rush to kill him. I challenge us to try understanding what produced him first then do whatever you think is necessary.

Conspiracy theorist will argue that the United States inflicted these casualties on themselves in an effort to bring in the New World Order. As if September 11, 2001 was not enough to justify announcing the conception of a New World Order. A world wherein you're right to privacy is secondary, and homeland security is primary. A New World Order that allows and welcomes big brother spying on its denizens. Others will contend that John Allen Muhammad and the younger suspect were programmed to kill by secret agents within the United States military. The Newsweek article in November 2002 mentioned the group in its special edition on the sniper. You will hear rumors of these two men being finance by Hamas, or Holy Jihad cadres. Muammar Qaddafi's name will probably come up as a possible supplier to the snipers in the future, in the minds of conspiracy theorist as they write books on the sniper case. A few people will forever think that the United States government framed the two so that the real killer could escape with $10 million. "You tell them that the sniper was caught like a duck in a noose." People have stated that they do not believe the law got their guy in spite of the overwhelming evidence found in the killer mobile. There is no way to control the various reactions and responses people will have whenever high profile crimes take place. The conjecturers will take to the streets. Distrust of law enforcement and government is growing all over America. Not too many people believe what is reported on the news. We have been told untruths more than enough, especially at election time!

Muammar Qaddafi remains suspect in the eyes of the Bush Administration. Today Mr. Qaddafi is doing everything in his power to unify the entire African Continent. This effort is not reported in your plutocratic newspapers. Use your Internet and other resources to research how the media is operated, who runs it, and what information they will allow to be propagated? You may also want to find books written by Muammar Qaddafi as he cross-examines globally racist practices.

Something about horrific events captures the imagination of men, and they create all kinds of wild stories to help them deal with the tragedy. A book is out in Europe claiming the World Trade Center attack never occurred, and that American Oligarchies are behind the criminal act, using automatic pilot to fly the planes into the Twin Towers. These reactions are not unprecedented. Look at all the books on the assassination of John Fitzgerald Kennedy. Hundreds of people will never believe that Lee Harvey Oswald pulled the trigger to the rifle that killed the young president. Some wonder if our own government had JFK killed to keep him from going ahead with the nuclear non-proliferation treaty. Jack Ruby made sure that you and I would never know the truth behind the Kennedy assassination. The bullet that took Oswald's life buried that secret for eternity. Oswald's demise closed the book on that revelation. From that moment onward only speculation would follow. Malcolm X's death has turned into a mystery too. Who really killed Brother Minister? Did the Central Intelligence Agency have anything to do with Malcolm's murder in New York on February 21, 1965? When so many people kill for so many reasons, from governments to individuals, it is hard to figure out the mindset that engenders the "psychology of killing."

John Allen Muhammad is not following the orders of some Anti-American outfit, Islamic group; nor are their actions reflective of the controversial Nation of Islam, their teachings, or doctrine. The Nation of Islam is a *peaceful organization* that does not even carry a pin-knife. And they do not act violently against anyone, unless they are attacked first. If they are molested in any way, they will not 'turn the other cheek.' If John Allen Muhammad was a martial arts instructor, he should have known the virtue of self-discipline and *proper conduct*. Martial arts consist of the oriental discipline that develops a person's spiritual attunement. The sniper or snipers actions did not exemplify genuine Islamic practice, nor did it represent martial arts. If he is guilty of the killings then he acted like a beast with rabies. His tarot card should have read: "Dear Minister Policeman, I am sickly evil, send me to a black liberation organization so I can get some real help." Senseless killing is the work of a deranged person, or an evil person. After 400 years of disenfranchisement many brothers are loosing their minds. Reparations and true opportunity is the only remedy, not violence. The Nation of Islam is trying to wake the brothers up. The Million-Man March was a clear effort to mobilize black men to be politically acclimated, family sensitive, and spiritually connected to one universal truth. Violence has never been taught, nor has it ever been the solution to fight against American Interest. Even when the Los Angeles police busted in the Temple, back in the 1960's, and outright killed a Muslim brother, the Honorable Elijah Muhammad said that violence was not the way to handle the situation. Malcolm X disagreed and felt that tit for tat was the emancipator. "What is good for the goose is good for the gander." There is a famous picture of Malcolm X looking out the window with rifle in hand. It was the *supreme wisdom* of Elijah Muhammad that kept the Nation of Islam from being the first Waco. You witnessed how our government dealt with white Christians that purchased guns for protection in Texas.

## True Members

The month of October is sacred to members of the *Lost and Found Tribe of Shabazz*. True members of the Nation of Islam would be preparing to celebrate The Honorable Elijah Muhammad's birth date, October 7. Those who follow Minister Louis Farrakhan would be celebrating both 'The Messengers' birth date and the upcoming anniversary of 'The Million Man March,' October 16. No true member would be loading a high-powered rifle and aiming the barrow towards innocent civilians.

## Weapons Are Forbidden

Guns are against the teachings, but some do go astray from the straight path. Just like Christianity there are many branches of The Nation of Islam. Some will not turn the other cheek. But this is true of most religions. George Bush is a Christian and he will drop a bomb on a village in a moments notice. Other Christians cannot bring themselves to kill under no circumstances. They would rather die like Jesus first. Different branches in the nation are no exception. Theological differences and philosophical conflict makes it somewhat difficult to mend the various branches. When charismatic leaders disagree, other branches grow from *the original tree of life*. When a tree is split down the middle, it falls on both sides, some seeds fall on fertile ground, and others land on rocks, while some choke themselves without ever realizing their full potential. "You can tell a good tree by the fruit it bears." And so it is.

## Innumerable Denominations

This should not surprise you with all the innumerable denominations in Christianity. You would not expect the Lutheran Church to throw away its doctrinal differences and accept the teachings of The Catholic Church. With all the various Islamic sects in America, none of the branches teach striking innocent people. Violence cannot be used to force one to accept Islam because 'there is no compulsion in Islam,' according to Prophet Mohammed (PBUH). Nor can violence be inflicted on innocuous people to settle the score over some personal domestic dispute, or some international grievance. You can only kill in self-defense.

## General Orders

The *general orders* mention no deliberate assaults or misuse of physical supremacy against innocent people, not even against the enemy. Suicide bombings are totally unacceptable, if you are a member of The Nation of Islam. Killing innocent people is not the way to usher in *Freedom, Justice, and Equality*. He, who takes a life, will be robbed of his life. If you live by the sword, then you will die by the same sword. Once you destroy the devil in you, you will see the god in someone else. In the teachings you cannot justify flagrant acts of violence against innocent people, and if you think this way you have been '*hoodwinked, bamboozled, and lead astray.*' Unprovoked acts of violence would make you a devil, not a god.

It is the same mentality that motivates American soldiers to kill innocent people overseas, in huts, poor towns, and villages out of their patriotism for 'god and country.' The mind can easily be programmed to think in a distorted manner. The right circumstances and unique psychological mindset can make almost anything possible. The Honorable Elijah Muhammad would say, "If you practice and teach violence, then you die in the same manner." If Malcolm X were living today, he would speak out against the actions of John Allen Muhammad after he heard all the facts surrounding the case. Malcolm X would not jump to conclusions. As a thinking man he would take into consideration some mental disturbances that may be affecting John's judgment and self-control. He would see whether or not John is an agent provocateur. Was he carrying out a military assignment? Was John on some medication, or had he taken some medication that had an adverse affect on his thinking? *Justice could mean looking at every situation with intelligence and open-mindedness and then making a wise decision that best fits what has been discovered in the investigation.*

### Persian Gulf War

As a Persian Gulf War Veteran Mr. John Allen Muhammad may be suffering from acute Post- Traumatic Stress Disorder. Your rush to judgment may send a disturbed man to his grave. History shows us that America will not hesitate to send mentally disturbed or retarded people to the electric chair. Nor do they have a problem with executing juveniles. Some states will kill a ten-year-old child. We are the only so-called civilized nation that practices Capital Punishment. All other civilized *western powers* have done away with Capital Punishment. All data shows that their crime rate has fallen significantly when compared to ours. In America, crime is on the rise in spite of our widespread and discriminatory practice of Capital Punishment. With the advent of DNA research many people are being cut loose after being falsely convicted. Let us go back to Maryland for a moment. There is one more thing I want you to consider. Everything I am sharing with you makes for good research.

## Montgomery County

Montgomery, County would be disproportionately affected by the crimes of the sniper or snipers. An inactive member of Minister Louis Farrakhan's group would be blamed for the brutal crimes. This embarrassment would be more devastating than the death of Malcolm X or the attempted murder of Dr. Khalid Abdul Muhammad in California. However, The Nation of Islam will survive the onslaught of media criticism just as the Vatican survived the murder of a Swiss Guard and his wife by another Swiss Guard years ago. You simply cannot reasonably hold leaders responsible for everything their troubled members do that leave the flock.

## George Lincoln Rockwell

George Lincoln Rockwell was murdered in a laundry mat by his close associate and it may have lowered the moral of his followers, but racism is alive and well in spite of his death. The World Wide Church of Christ, founded by Michael Hale continues to teach his doctrine of Racial Holy War (Rahawa) right here in Confederate Richmond. A few years ago one of their racist members went on a killing spree in Indiana, Illinois, killing four or five people, before committing suicide. Overall, the Nation of Islam has a better record of personal conduct in its ranks, undoubtedly better than the Catholic Church. We all saw what took place in Texas with the Bishops this year. No one is talking about investigating the Vatican, or criticizing the so-called Holy Father. Pedophile priest raping and molesting innocent children and no one points the finger at 'The Pope,' I beg your pardon!

## Logical Responsibility

You cannot hold the Pope responsible for every perverted priest accused of molesting unsuspecting children in the diocese or senseless crimes committed by them. However, the Pope can excommunicate them once they are found guilty. Nor can Michael Hale or Minister Louis Farrakhan be made responsible for the negative outburst of one of their members. Just as Jews cannot be judged when a rabbi is accused of killing his wife or robbing a bank. Why even the 'Son of Sam' was Jewish! Despite his nationality his actions does not reflect the whole Jewish group. That would be like jailing President Bush when a citizen of the United States commits a crime overseas. As long as men co-exist among other men there will be killings and law-breakers. Aggression is as natural as cold in the winter. And yet, aggression must be controlled and regulated by law, custom, and practice. A sport is an excellent way to regulate and control aggression. Killings are not right and will not be tolerated among civilized men. The question is what will turn a conscious man into a foolish murderer? John Allen Muhammad was intelligent enough to study with *the fruit* at some point in his life, so what sent him running in the wrong direction? Hopefully, someone will ask this question during the court proceedings.

## The Bushmaster XM-15

A total of six people would die from one shot delivered from a Bushmaster XM-15 .223- caliber rifle in the Maryland district. Later officials would claim the over-representation of dead bodies in their jurisdiction should give them the right to try the cases first. Louisiana and Washington State, among other areas would want their share in the prosecution of the most feared sniper or snipers the United States ever seen. Will white cinema make movies glorifying these crimes like they do for white killers? You have heard of Frank and Jesse James all of your life? When one is thinking about the insanity of glorifying crime or criminal behavior, it seems to only apply when glorifying black killers. There is no paradox with glorification of crime when the criminals are white. Even Spike Lee understood there would be no problem making a movie on the 'Son of Sam.' We have all heard of the escape from Alcatraz Prison, but what about the largest escape from death row in American history? When blacks outsmart, out maneuver, and outwit white folk movie deals are ignored. Directors will be somewhat reluctant to make a film on John Allen Muhammad. He does not deserve a film, but it may teach us something about black rage. Hesitantly, we must admit that it is now a part of our history. Shameful as it may be to black scholars, it is written as the worse sniper case in American History. Historians write about Adolf Hitler, not because they approve of his sick mind or actions, but solely because he helped to shape the twentieth century. John Allen Muhammad will be remembered as a Black Muslim and convert to the Nation of Islam. It is necessary that we begin to understand the man and the times that produced him. Violence is becoming normal to many urban youth. We can address it now, or suffer from it tomorrow.

## Youthful Rebellion

What looks to the *normal mind* to be belligerency, appears to the troubled youth like heaven. Rebellion and the thought of emancipation from parental authority fascinate youth. Youth is a dangerous time for adolescents, psychologists are aware of this. But what happens when an older man loses control of his life and is disenfranchised of his parental responsibility? Better yet, what will he feel if all that he has worked for disappears in a matter of months? Cultural Shock sets in and rages deep, bubbling in the soul. You fight to save the vital interest of your Country, only to lose your home, Job, and business, all that you hold dear! If you are unable to maintain your sanity and composed state of mind, war may be the answer. But whom will you declare it on? John declared it on America, if he is guilty.

## Inexcusable Barbarity

I do not excuse his whirlwind of anger that took the lives of so many moderate people, but I understand his conflict. I have read where white men have killed their families when they felt the pressure of social misfortune, like unemployment, separation, significant lose of finances, and institutional disrespect. Susan Smith drowned her children in a lake when her husband left her and then blamed a black man of kidnapping her children. Of course, the police believed her in put an all-points-bulletin on every dark skinned Negro in the area. Another white woman killed five of her offspring years later. Desperation in the white community is somehow understood more so than in the inner city. I do realize that unwarranted violence cannot be reasoned away. I am not trying to excuse the awful acts of a coward sniper. I am pointing to a deeper social issue that I feel will not be addressed. John Allen Muhammad will probably be put to death and the ingredients that manufactured him will duplicate him in some other metropolitan area. He will be judged in the same place where Billy Taylor was Judged hundreds of years ago, and put to death at Greenville Correctional Center if found guilty.

## Criminal Ambiguity

When white men like Ted Bundy and Jeffrey Dahmer make national notoriety the news media call them intelligent and charming. Book deals are made and Hollywood makes millions depicting them as victims of some inner conflict. Charles Manson has a fan club and several movies and book deals. Not so with so-called minority felons. The most a black killer can look for is a segment on some discovery channel showing how stupid he was. On the other hand, white men make it to the big screen for their violent conduct. We all know that moviegoers look upon criminals ambiguously. Future historians will wonder why so much emphasis was placed on sensationalizing mental *slavery*, *suffering*, and *death*; and not enough time on curing social diseases like AIDS and illiteracy. *Freedom* can only be obtained if we face our challenges and move towards *peace* and *equality*. No criminal act deserves to be overvalued in a society pledged by transgression, mental disturbance, and easy access to guns and ammunition. How was John Allen Muhammad able to purchase a gun after a complaint against him for Domestic Violence? And how was the gun taken aboard a Grey Hound Bus post-911? I guess this means Homeland Security is hopeless anytime a man can kill in one state, board a public bus, and travel to the Capitol without any suspicion.

## Jurisdiction

Each *jurisdiction* wants to inflict lethal force on the accused to satisfy the desire of the people, seeking revenge is acceptable when the people are offended. When the populace is afraid to travel to work, go to a park, visit the Mall, or simply take an afternoon stroll, something drastic must be done to reassure them that life has returned to normal. Normalcy is hard to reestablish after body bags pave the streets and we are forced to see them on the evening news. Wondering if our loved ones are safe today, or if we are safe tomorrow! Our sense of security is violated. If you destroy the culprit the people will feel somewhat safe. Violence for violence is the formula used to restore confidence in the minds of the people. Kill those who kill and ignore those who need help sustaining themselves in a complex society. That is the policy of *The Machine*.

## The Machine

The Machine uses most of its energy and powers making sure rich people stay rich. Never mind those who must live at places like the Light House Mission in Bellingham, Washington; they are considered failures, social misfits, and the underprivileged. The Machine will deal with them when the social misfit gets tired of his misery and strike back at society through crime. The Machine will then recognize him or her and make them infamous, not famous. The Machines course of action, both Republican and Democrat alike, is always palliative not curative when it comes to the suffering masses. Issues like food, shelter, and clothing are placed on the back burner during *Twenty-first century* elections, and terrorism and crime move to the front of National debate.

To call something a 'Machine' is to remove its human potential, and it specifies your relationship to it. You become an automated cog, or more simply put, a replaceable part of the machine. You may feel like a cog in 'The Machine,' which regulates your life. Criminals feel that this relationship is intolerable and they fight the inanimate object with violence. Serial killers feel separate from 'The Machine' and they no longer want to play the rich man's game.

## Meager Existence

When poor people get fed up with their meager existence and frustration turns to anxiety, crime is the final outcome. Too many brothers have fought wars for this Country only to return home with little or nothing to live for. Their skills are obsolete and the weak or unstable economy no longer needs them in the workplace.

## Corporate Elite's

Not to mention the continuous robbery they suffer from so-called *corporate elites* who exploit and take millions of dollars and amass great wealth in a selfish manner. The wealth is gained at the expense and detriment of the poor. It is these realities that have the potential of making violent criminals feel justified. The mind has great difficulty sorting out this contradiction, but it is helped by a media enterprise that produces sensational reports and stories designed to capture wide audiences and shape peoples opinion on any given subject. These reports never erase the poverty line that causes one to feel like an outcast.

## Societal Conflicts

Even with these societal conflicts there are some crimes that are intolerable and the state is expected to act swiftly. Subsequently, the global media apparatus would cover the spree killings like a Presidential Inauguration. Killing right before election time is just like signing your own death warrant and petitioning a swarm of media to make sure you die violently! One television commentator said she wanted the accused to be tortured severely until they die. She now has the mind of a killer whether she knows it or not. The message will be "Predators must be taken out" and the state is certified to carry out the sentence with public approval. Every major network will echo the above demand as the killer is hunted down like the coward he or she is. But the social neglect that produce African-American serial killers is never addressed.

White people kill for different reasons then blacks. Most of your white serial killers are disturbed over a feeling of sexual inadequacy, whereas, black serial killings stems from economic disparity and lack of social control. Black criminals feel a strong sense of alienation from mainstream society. They feel justified attacking private property, especially when they own nothing in the richest Country on earth. I am not referring to the bourgeois class that joins secret societies, fraternities, and churches' to establish a support system to guide them, and help them through life. This report is an exegesis on the ghettoized black man that has *'nothing to lose but his chains.'* Since the white man will not pay him reparations then he will take back his share of the pie. In his mind all black folk who make it are *'sell outs.'* His question to them is 'how did you make it without me?' Let us return to Virginia now.

### Governor Mark R. Warner

In Virginia, Governor Mark R. Warner was scheduled to appear on WRVA, a Richmond radio station, to stamp his voice of approval to try the suspects in a Virginia court. He knows that it makes for good politics to hint at destroying *'enemies of the state.'* When he runs for President one day, he can remind the *'conservative voters'* of his willingness to kill for the people. If any state can carry out the execution once Muhammad and Malvo are found guilty of these ferocious crimes, Virginia can. Eighty-six people have been executed in Virginia since the 1976 reinstatement of the death penalty, and only three people in Maryland during that same period have been put to death. Texas and Florida have a notorious history of potassium chloride injection too. A few weeks ago Florida killed a white woman for being a serial killer. If a crime committed by John Allen Muhammad pops up in Florida the fight over who kills him will get very interesting indeed. Florida loves to count the black men they kill, even though they have a problem counting the black men who vote. The black man is constantly reminded of his servitude in white America, and the Florida voting episode during the last election did not help matters. Our rage is suppressed for survival adaptation reasons. We dare not rock the boat! The ugliness of America is raised at election time.

## Negative Campaigns

Politicians love tragic events, like crime and punishment, at election time. Democratic candidate for Congress, Anne Sumers, used the Sniper Case to put down her opponent, and she quickly produced negative campaign advertisements to be shown on local television. You would think this illegal since he has not been convicted of anything yet. These advertisements are designed to make her opponent somehow responsible for what the sniper or snipers did. Her tactic reminded me of the Willie Horton fiasco that prevented Michael S. Dukakis, another democratic candidate from winning his bid for presidency in 1988. The democrats seem to mimic the evil methods of the republicans. They think the people are not intelligent enough to distinguish the difference. It amazes me what grown folk will do to win the minds and votes of emotional people.

## Black Criminals

Perhaps, you may find it mind-boggling that both instances mentioned above involved black criminals. The history of our country illustrates the exploitation and over generalization of black crime directly, and indirectly, to maintain *white supremacy* through fear-driven elections. The sniper case will be used to tighten the immigration dilemma, the gun laws, and the national database for guns where each gun is registered, as well as turn more people towards approving capital punishment. If a case could be argued to support the death penalty, this sniper situation is the one to use. I get the feeling that if you are against the death penalty, this is not the time to voice your opposition. You might be accused of having *Anti-American sentiments.*

## Never Considered Innocent

The onslaught of the media has preconditioned our minds to view the suspects as guilty before trial. Mr. Douglas Gansler, Montgomery County States Attorney went on television arguing his case to try the killers in Maryland based on the number of casualties, not the guilt or innocence of the accused. The philosophical and legal idea that 'you are considered innocent until proven guilty' was thrown out of the equation. The bearded Mr. Robert Cleary, Former Federal prosecutor also feels that Montgomery County suffered the greatest impact from the crimes. The current moratorium on the death penalty in Maryland is what makes prosecutors reluctant to allow the primary or initial trial to start there. With all the media outlets driving home the guilt of the suspects, where in America will they find an impartial jury of their peers or Judge not shaping his political career? The other reason Maryland is disfavored is due to a law on the books that preclude the execution of juveniles in their state. I find it troubling that the main discussion is on who will kill the accused, instead of political and legal dialogue focusing on the non-prejudicial process of America's Criminal Justice System! This kind of unbalanced media reporting has the potential of being dangerous to civilized nations.

## Taste of Blood

You would think gamblers were placing bets on pit-bull fights as spectators craved the taste of blood, hoping one dog would kill the other, while standing behind the death chamber, placing bets, drinking, and hungry for death, waiting for cash. The fight among jurisdictions to have a shot at trying the killers first would seem just as truculent as the killings were bloody. Jurisdiction must be established if the case can be successfully prosecuted. In the final analysis, each state wanted to put the sniper or snipers to death once they were apprehended. Even the federal government would join the scrimmage.

## Jockeying to Kill

Prosecutors from Montgomery, Alabama to Hanover, Virginia would jockey for a position to politicize this spree killing, especially as November the fifth approached. Who would *show, place, or win* as the courts positioned them to judge the accused at the gate of white justice? The field where the race for punishment would be run might need to be cleaned several times due to the political dung all over the tracks.

## Speech of Politicians

It is important that the public learn to connect the speech of politicians to the operation and application of law. "The moral weight" to prosecute the case should go to the place that was affected the most, according to Cynthia Alksne. Even the voters want to see justice served and it looks good seeing public officials crave the blood of whoever was responsible for the massacre. "We hate it when people kill, but we love to kill people who kill," an anonymous person once said after witnessing a Christian white lady die of lethal injection in a Texas prison during the Bush Administration. Her execution lifted Governor George Bush's approval rating greatly and guaranteed his presidency in the next election.

## Political Mobility

George Bush, the younger was governor at that time and would not convert her sentence to life imprisonment, even though she claimed to be a Christian. She would literally dance in front of the camera days before her execution, but her pomposity and preaching was not enough to save her life. A lot of media coverage was drawn to her conviction and execution. Her death became a political victory for the younger Bush's walk to the White House. If he is capable of carrying out the execution of a white woman, what does this convey to the public about his ability to allow many black men, women, and juveniles to die on the infamous bed that is shaped like a cross? He did not just allow a white woman to die, but a white Christian woman! You should wonder what this suggests for Black Muslim criminals, or black Muslims accused of multiple murders near the White House.

## The Pentagon's Efforts

The Pentagon took law enforcement aboard its global imaging space craft for training; this plane is capable of reading the back of a cigarette pack from long ranges without the holder of the cigarette pack ever realizing that he or she is being watch at all. It has the ability to trace sound from handguns and riffles alike, and it can register the heat from your body on a cold winter day.

Thermo-detecting equipment that follow the heat from escaping suspects and sends outlines of their fleeing bodies back to the plane for identification and tracking data is quickly relayed to authorities.

## Posse Comitatus

Law Enforcement officers had to board the plane as a 'trainee' in order not to violate the posse comitatus rule of law. Civilians are not to be sought after by the military, but the sniper case was an exception. A few legal terms would have to be twisted to justify the operation. But the operation would be carried out with precision and governmental approval. The President must declare a National Emergency in order to send in the troops. He would not do this in the sniper case. In the course of the Watts riot over Rodney Kings thrashing from wild and unruly police the army was sent out to hunt down civilians who stole and vandalized private property. The sniper spree would mobilize cops on the ground and in the air. This hunt was huge! However, it was never named a national emergency. I am intimating the way in which this case was handled by law enforcement and the different agencies involved. The event of the October killings will be studied by Criminal Justice students and governments the world over. Every one wants to know how the sniper or snipers got away so long and evaded arrest, even with all of America's high-tech machinery and equipment aimed at the areas where the crimes concentrated? Is American military personal bragging about its ability to 'protect and serve' the general public, when in fact, primitive warfare, like stabbings, beatings, and sniper assault has proven to outsmart high-tech equipment? Can a determined criminal outmaneuver the Pentagon? If so, what will the Washington sniper teach America's determined enemies? Enemies like the ones who flew the planes into The

World Trade Center, the building that was rented for 99 years by a rich quasi-Jew named Larry Silverstein.

## Was Global Terrorist Watching?

The fear now is that global terrorist organizations saw how to bring America to its knees. They are probably saying amongst themselves: "You strike slowly, with patient, unpredictable, and at random targets. Use the main arteries to blend in and out of the populace, hide, and wait a few hours, days, perhaps months, and then strike again. Never communicate with law enforcement and only leave misleading clues. Keep the profilers guessing and running up and down the wrong tree. Hit targets that create the best psychological unease in the population, like teachers, school children, businessmen, shoppers, and lawn maintenance workers, as well as those who travel along the Interstate highways. All of these targets are exposed and forever unprotected."

## Point of Exhaustion

The sniper or snipers main aim was to defocus the populace and tax law enforcement to the point of exhaustion. Law Enforcement knows that it would have taken longer to catch the suspects if they had not communicated with the criminals in some way. The channel of communication between law enforcement and the criminal, or criminals, had to stay open. This had to be accomplished through the media and telephone. In the end, the telephone calls to tip lines, the priest, and CNN from the snipers is what would solve the case. The biggest lead would come from one of the snipers bragging about a liquor store murder in Montgomery County, Alabama.

Self-hatred is the main motivator for violence in the communities I have lived in. In fact, community is not even a proper descriptive word to best identify the customs of black neighborhoods, especially those that exist below the poverty line. Black districts are part and parcel of American society. However, no one responds to our pain, suffering, and neglect. It is only when white peoples interest are assaulted that attention is paid to the impact of violence. Focus groups have been warning America of the widespread increase of violence for well over thirty years, but no one is listening. I guess we will have to wait until the Court Case in October for more information on the "Psychology of Killing." From October 2, 2002 until the death of Ken, the killings formed a five-pointed star, an ancient pagan symbol. You tell me what is going on in the mind of the esoteric killer? The author of this book will continue the investigation into the sniper case until the family of Kenneth H. Bridges can find the true reason why he was murdered, or until the community is satisfied that genuine justice was served. May YAHWEH continue to bless the family of this great man?

And so it is!

Dare to Struggle!
Dare to Win!

Forward ever, backwards never!

# ABOUT THE AUTHOR

Eric Penn was raised in Watts, Los Angeles, Santa Ana, and Richmond, Virginia. Most of his childhood was consumed in detention homes, group homes, and foster care. His early adult years were consumed in Virginia's maximum security prisons. Eight and one-half years of his life was spent around notorious killers, rapist, and other criminals. Four and one-half years was exhausted in solitary confinement hearing psychotic individuals' brag through the air vents about heinous crimes. Mr. Penn decided to study the psychotic nature of deranged criminals and turned his cell into a university. Through a process of erudition, eclectic studies, and careful observation, Mr. Penn discovered a unique thread that ties criminals together. The most notorious cases possessed a strange hatred towards anyone in authority. All inmates were suspicious of the American government and felt they were victims of a larger conspiracy. Every once in awhile books would make its way to solitary confinement and inmates would debate its content. Books such as "Behold a pale horse" by William Cooper would be discussed into the wee hours of the night. The most conscious inmates were ultra-rebellious and the Correctional Officers approached them with caution. Mr. Penn was paroled after serving his term and immediately started writing his first book: Children of Chaos: Breaking the cycle of family and social dysfunction. Today, Mr. Penn works for a non-profit organization as a Family Case Manager teaching parents how to nurture and raise healthy children. Mr. Penn has a unique way of solving what he terms "esoteric crimes," using psychology, media outlets, history, and current sociology to uncover deeper clues within horrible crimes.

Printed in the United States
151652LV00001B/9/A

9 781420 870060